Robert Dwyer Joyce

Ballads, romances, and songs

Robert Dwyer Joyce

Ballads, romances, and songs

ISBN/EAN: 9783742831552

Manufactured in Europe, USA, Canada, Australia, Japa

Cover: Foto ©Thomas Meinert / pixelio.de

Manufactured and distributed by brebook publishing software
(www.brebook.com)

Robert Dwyer Joyce

Ballads, romances, and songs

BALLADS,

ROMANCES, AND SONGS.

BY

ROBERT DWYER JOYCE.

> "She is a rich and rare land;
> Oh! she's a fresh and fair land;
> She is a dear and rare land—
> This native land of mine".
> THOMAS DAVIS.

DUBLIN:
JAMES DUFFY, 7 WELLINGTON QUAY;
AND
22 PATERNOSTER ROW, LONDON.
1861.

J. F. FOWLER, PRINTER,
3 CROW STREET, DAME STREET,
DUBLIN.

TO GRACIE

This volume is affectionately dedicated

BY

THE AUTHOR.

PREFACE.

Of the Ballads and Songs contained in this volume, it may be proper to say a few words.

In them I have designed to do for Ireland that which she would not have lacked had her old language remained dominant, and her customs, so favourable to bardic literature, inviolate, or modified by friendly hands alone. Her romantic legends would have been cared for, and the high feats and chivalrous deeds which illumine her story enshrined in poetry. At the present time, however, there remain to us, in Irish, few poems of any value, save those which treat of times remote; the wars and cruel laws which have troubled our history since the extension of the Pale, having to some extent either hindered the inspiration of the Bards, or caused their productions to be lost for ever. I have endeavoured, in another tongue, to supply their absence, with what fortune each reader will judge. The legends and fragments of song, dear to the peasantry of the glenns and mountains—tenacious of old things—have been long familiar, and served as guides: in some instances, I have adopted stray lines and old verses, beautiful but incomplete, and mated them to the martial, pathetic, and humorous airs which the people love.

In conclusion, I am not forgetful how much and how well others have before me wrought to popularize the chivalry and romance of our native land.

R. D. J.

CONTENTS.

BALLADS.

Crossing the Blackwater,	77
Dunboy,	32
Little Thomas,	18
Mary Lombard,	86
Maud of Desmond,	93
Mary's sweetheart,	153
Romance of the Golden Spurs,	99
Rose Condon,	64
Romance of the Golden Helmet,	9
Romance of the Black Robber,	22
Romance of the Stone Coffin,	56
Romance of the Banner,	60
Romance of the Fairy Wand,	44
Rossnalee,	74
Romance of Meergal and Garmon,	79
Sir Domnall,	106
The Green Dove and the Raven,	16
The White Ladye,	36
The Dying Ballad-singer,	20
The Siege of Clonmel,	24
The Fairy Mill,	30
The Two Galloglachs,	21
The Battle of Kiltili,	40
The Battle of Knockinoss,	34
The Spalpeen,	90
The Lady of the Sea,	144
The Dying Warrior,	104
The Templar Knight,	50
The Battle of Benburb,	13
The Enchanted Warhorse,	128
The Baron and the Miller,	114
The Well of the Omen,	126
The Sack of Dunbui,	138
The Battle of Thurles,	71

CONTENTS.

The Pilgrim,	135
The Taking of Armagh,	120
The Battle of the Raven's Glen,	161
The Death of O'Donnell,	148
The Burning of Kilcoleman,	96
Tyrrell's Pass,	155

SONGS.

Along with my love I'll go,	189
Annie de Clare	235
Allisdrum's march at the battle of Knockinoss,	195
Alley Kelly O!	201
Among the fragrant hay,	298
Asthoreen Machree,	278
Adieu, lovely Mary,	291
Brave Donall,	226
Come, all you maids, where'er you be,	271
Donall na Greine,	204
Diarmid Mór,	200
Donal O'Keeffe's lament,	182
Eileen's lament for Gerald,	264
Fanny,	303
Fair Helen of the dell,	215
Fainge an lae,	237
Far away,	174
Fair Maidens' beauty will soon fade away,	231
Fanny Clair,	246
Fair Kate of Glenanner,	211
Fairest and rarest,	270
Fineen the Rover,	205
Glenara,	275
Gra Gal Ban,	239
Gra Gal Machree,	188
I loved a maid,	254
I still am a rover,	227
I sit on the Hold of Moyallo,	220
I thought she loved me dearly,	184
I wish I sat by Grena's side,	259
I built me a bower,	230
I never can forget,	178
I'm fourteen years old upon Sunday,	292
Johnny's return,	251
Johnny Dunlea,	282
Jessy Brien,	255

CONTENTS.

Lament of Garodh Earla,	167
My boat,	165
Mary, the pride of the west,	273
My Irish girl,	290
My love is on the river,	274
My steed was weary,	173
My true love,	266
Mary Earley,	199
My heart is wild,	169
My true love bright,	186
My first love,	219
My Anna's eyes,	208
Maryanne,	218
Merrily, merrily playing,	213
My Mary,	223
Margaret,	254
My flower of flowers,	203
My love is at my side,	301
Margead Bān,	276
Oh! fair shines the sun on Glenara,	207
Over the hills and far away,	279
O'Sullivan's flight,	250
Over the morning-dew,	294
Roving Brian O'Connell,	260
Song of Galloping O'Hogan,	302
Song of Sarsfield's trooper,	267
Song of Trén the fairy,	224
Song of the forest fairy,	212
Song,	252
Sweet Glengariff's water,	297
The flame that burned so brightly,	263
The withered rose,	280
The jolly companie,	284
The march out of Limerick,	236
The green ribbon,	233
The wind that shakes the barley,	244
The mountain ash,	175
There is a tree in Darra's wood,	229
The Drinan Dhun,	216
The blind girl of Glenore,	209
There is a stream,	181
The student,	172
The cannon,	170
The red lusmore,	187
The little bird,	196
The outlaw of Kilmore,	192

The locks of amber,	183
The ensign and his banner,	176
The coming bridal,	243
The Cailin Rue,	232
The cock and the sparrow,	179
The forsaken,	258
The rapparee's horse and sword,	222
The flower that ne'er shall fade,	169
The siege of Limerick,	214
The yellow hair,	206
The spring of the year,	190
The mountains high,	166
This maid of mine,	204
The first night I was married,	286
The wanderer,	268
The lasses of Ireland,	248
The merry Christmas fire,	185
The stormy sea shall flow in,	253
The Brigade's hurling match,	288
The summer is come,	293
The advice,	262
The boys of Wexford,	295
The saddest breeze,	300
The joy-bells,	282
Will of the Gap,	167
Whatever wind is blowing,	217
Willy Brand,	247

BALLADS.

ROMANCE OF THE GOLDEN HELMET.

I.

One glorious Easter even,
   Under the mountain tree,
A young knight sat bereaven,
   A-gazing up and down,—
Oh! wearily and drearily
Along the plains looked he,
   And up the summits brown.

II.

The birds were singing sweetly
   From the wild rowan grove,
The dun deer gambolled fleetly
   Beside the upland rills;
Yet wearily and drearily
He thought upon his love,
   Young Bride of the castled hills.

III.

His wolf hound by him lying
   Looked up into his face,
As though he read the flying
   Thoughts of his master's brain,—
How wearily, when drearily,
Through the brain's little space,
   Speeds thought's black train!

IV.

"Around my love's hoar dwelling"—
　'Twas thus Sir Brian said—
"The Norman host is swelling,
　And I a banished man;—
Oh! wearily and drearily
My mournful days have sped,
　Under the outlaw's ban!"

V.

Just then a white fawn darted
　Out from the rowan screen,
And up the wolf-hound started,
　And after her away,
And suddenly, oh! suddenly
Under the copses green
　Soon vanished they!

VI.

Beside a cave's hoar portal
　The wolf-hound lost his chase;—
Oh! was the white fawn mortal
　His keen eyes thus to blind?
Yet eagerly, oh! eagerly,
He still pursued the trace
　Through the cave like the wind!

VII.

Now came the sunset gleaming
　O'er haunted crag and dell,—
The young knight stays his dreaming,
　And looks once more around;
'Till eagerly, oh! eagerly,
Across the silent fell,
　Cometh his brave wolf-hound,

VIII.

In his mouth a helmet golden
  He'd found in th' ancient cave,
With a scroll decayed and olden
  Fastened beside the crest—
Who'll bear me, who'll wear me,
Shall have an army brave
  To do at his behest!

IX.

Sir Brian placed the helmet
  His plumèd cap instead,
And scarce had cried, "Oh! well met,
  My fenceless head and thou!"
When suddenly, oh! suddenly
He heard an army's tread
  Over the mountain's brow!

X.

And quickly filed before him
  A thousand mounted men;
High in the twilight o'er him
  Their gilded banners sail,
And gallantly, oh! gallantly
They rode in that wild glen,
  All in their glittering mail!

XI.

One led unto Sir Brian
  A mighty milk-white steed,
And he has mounted high on
  The antique saddle-tree;
And eagerly, oh! eagerly
All cried, "In thy great need
  Oh! now we'll follow thee!"

XII.

Away Sir Brian dashes
   With those wierd warriors all:
The craggy road-way flashes
   Beneath their horse-hoofs' bound,
'Till rushingly, oh! rushingly,
They speed nigh his true love's wall,
   By the Norman leaguered round.

XIII.

Behind Sir Brian kept they,
   Their proud plumes dancing high;
With brave Sir Brian swept they
   Upon the Norman crew,
And fearfully, oh! fearfully
Rose their ancient battle cry,
   Till every man they slew!

XIV.

His love came forth to meet him
   Beneath the midnight star,
His mountain friends to greet him,
   And those wierd warriors all,
Joyfully, oh! joyfully,
All crossed the fortress bar,
   And feasted in the hall.

XV.

Till morn's white planet lit them
   These champions could not wait;
The milk-white charger with them
   Towards the lone hills they bore;
Gallantly, oh! gallantly
They rode from the castle gate,
   And ne'er were looked on more!

XVI.

Long in that ancient castle,
 'Neath the gray Cummeragh's head,
Bright over feast and wassail
 That golden helmet shone,
And joyfully, oh! joyfully
These lovers twain were wed,
 Ere the next morn was gone!*

THE BATTLE OF BENBURB.
A.D. 1646.

I.

O'er the hills of Benburb rose the red beam of day,
Gleaming bright from our foemen in battle array;
But as brightly again 'mid the greenwoods below
Shone it back from the troops of our brave Owen Roe.

II.

Munroe had his thousands arrayed at his back,
With their Puritan mantles, steel morion, and jack,
And with him Ardes, Blayney, and Conway had come,
To cut Irish throats at the tuck of the drum!

III.

And who with O'Neill on that morn drew the brand?
Bold hearts as e'er beat by the Blackwater strand;
Sir Phelim, brave chief, with the bosom of fire,
O'Donnell, MacSweeny, and gallant Maguire.

---

* The tradition of the enchanted warriors is not confined to one part of Ireland. The peasantry of the Cummeragh valleys say that a troop of those ancient and spell-bound warriors may frequently be seen at night performing their evolutions on the wild mountain tracks, and in the rocky cooms near their dwellings.

IV.

From Derry's wild woodlands, from Main's sounding
    tide,
From Leitrim and Longford, chiefs came to our side,
And stern in the front, with his sabre in hand,
Stood bold Miles the Slasher, the pride of our band.*

V.

The foemen at morn crossed the Blackwater's wave,
Where O'Ferrall's five hundred a hot welcome gave;
But soon to our lines came his band pouring in,
Just to tell us the news of Kinnard's wild ravine.

VI.

Thus we kept all the noon the lean Scotsmen at play,
Though we thought of their forays and burned for
    the fray;
For our chief bade us wait 'till the eve had begun,
Then rush on the foe with our backs to the sun!

VII.

Then down to our front with his chiefs spurred he
    fast,—
"My brave men! the day of our weakness is past:
We have hearts now as firm as our sires had before,
When Bagnall they slew by the Blackwater shore!

VIII.

Hark! their cannon the foe for our columns have set!
Strike! and have them to play 'mid their own
    columns yet;
For God and green Erin sure and stern be your blow,
As ye fight in my path!" said our brave Owen Roe.

---

    * Maolmordha Mac Sweeny—commonly called Miles the
Slasher, from his wonderful strength and bravery.

IX.

Hurrah for the Red Hand! And on to a man,
Horse and foot, poured we down like a storm in
    their van,
Where they listed a sermon to strengthen their zeal,
And a sermon we gave them—the point of our steel!

X.

The Slasher looked round as we closed in the fight—
"Ho! Sir Phelim", he called, "reap your harvest
    ere night!"
Then he dashed at the foe with his long heavy blade,
And, *mavrone*, what a lane through their columns he
    made!

XI.

There was panic before us and panic beside,
As their horsemen fled back in a wild broken tide,
And we swept them along by the Blackwater shore
Till we reddened its deep tide with Sassenach gore!

XII.

Few foemen escaped on that well-stricken day;
O'er hillock and moorland by thousands they lay;
Fierce Blayney had fallen where he charged by the
    fen—
'Twas a comfort he slept by the side of his men!

XIII.

A kern by the river held something on high;—
"Saint Columb! is it thus that the Sassenachs fly?
Perchance 'tis my coolun which they clipped long
    ago,—
Mille Gloria! the rough wig of flying Munroe!"

XIV.

And we took from the foe, ere that calm twilight fall,
Their horses and baggage, and banners and all,
Then we sat by our watch-fires, and drank in the
    glow
Merry healths to our leaders and brave Owen Roe!

THE GREEN DOVE AND THE RAVEN.

I.

There was a dove with wings of green,
    Glistening o'er so radiantly,
With head of blue and golden sheen,
    All sad and wearily
Sitting two red blooms between
    On lovely Barna's wildwood tree.

II.

There was a letter 'neath its wing,
    Written by a fair ladye,
Safely bound with silken string
    So light and daintily,
And in that letter was a ring,
    On lovely Barna's wildwood tree.

III.

There was a raven, black and drear,
    Stained with blood all loathsomely,
Perched upon the branches near,
    Croaking mournfully,
And he said, "Oh! dove, what bring'st thou here,
    To lovely Barna's wildwood tree?"

IV.

"I'm coming from a ladye gay,
   To the young heir of sweet Glenore,
His ring returned, it is to say
   She'll never love him more,—
Alas the hour! alas the day!
   By murmuring Funcheon's fairy shore!"

V.

"Oh! dove, outspread thy wings of green:
   I'll guide thee many a wildwood o'er,
I'll bring thee where I last have seen
   The young heir of Glenore,
Beneath the forest's sunless screen,
   By murmuring Funcheon's fairy shore!"

VI.

O'er many a long mile did they flee,
   The dove, the raven stained with gore,
And found beneath the Murderer's tree
   The young heir of Glenore,—
A bloody, ghastly corpse was he,
   By murmuring Funcheon's fairy shore!

VII.

"Go back! go back! thou weary dove,—
   To the cruel maid tell o'er and o'er,
He's Death's and mine, her hate or love
   Can never reach him more—
To his ice-cold heart in Molagga's grove,
   By murmuring Funcheon's fairy shore!"

LITTLE THOMAS.

I.

'Neath the towers of old Ardfinnan, by the broad ford's mossy stone,
Down sat the little Thomas, and thus he made his moan,—
"He has perished, he has perished, oh! my chieftain young and brave,
And my father too sleeps with him, underneath the rushing wave!

II.

Many hearts for John of Desmond* thro' the Mumhan valleys pine,
But there beats not one amongst them half so desolate as mine,—
I, the little page, that ever by my dear dead lord would stay,—
I, the orphan lone, whose father hath perished here to-day!"

III.

Died the purple of the sunset from the blue and watery sky,
Rose the moon in clear white splendour o'er the peakëd mountains high,
But the little page sat weeping still beside the ford's gray stone,
And to the waters sweeping thus again he made his moan.

---

* John, the young Earl of Desmond, was drowned at the Ford of Ardfinnan, on his return from a foray, in the year 1399.

IV.

"Woe is me! that they have perished; here my home, until I find
A master like the Desmond, a lord so good and kind"—
Looked he on the curling water with a sudden throb of fear,
For the Desmond stood before him in the moonlight cold and clear!

V.

On his limbs the battle harness, on his head bright helm and plume,
But pale, pale were his features, marked that morn with youth's fair bloom.
"Stay thy lorn and bitter weeping, oh! my little page", he said,
"For beneath the waters sweeping it has waked the early dead!

VI.

The good sword that I gave thee on our last victorious day,
It shall carve thy path to glory, if bright honour light the way.—
One little maid there dwelleth by the green shores of the Lee,
Only she shall love thee fonder than my constant love for thee!"

VII.

Vanished the phantom warrior in the cold light of the moon,
And the little page now heareth but the Suir's loud thundering tune;

Swift he rusheth from the water, swift he springeth
  on his steed,
And thro' the moonlit forest is he gone with lightning speed!

VIII.

Ten springs more have decked the mountains, and it
  is a morn of May;
Knightly spurs the page now weareth, for bright
  honour lit his way;
Before the bridal altar with a happy heart stands he,
And his bride is that fair maiden by the green shore
  of the Lee!

THE DYING BALLAD SINGER.

I.

Oh! Thady dear, the way is long,
  My heart and feet are sore and weary,
I'll never sing another song
  In tented Fair or Patron cheery;
But since the day I met with you,
  I never envied lord or lady;
No care, nor woe, nor joy I knew
  That was not shared by Rovin' Thady.

II.

It seems that now but days have flown
  Since first you bade to me "Good-morrow",
Though many a year is past and gone,—
  Ah! many a year of want and sorrow.
It was a sunny morn in June,
  The winds and waves were sweetly playing,
And you struck up your favourite tune,
  "The Piper in the meadow straying!"

III.

Since th' hour I ran from home away,
    Oh! many a pang my heart has riven:
The worst of all was that Fair day,
    I saw my brother at Knockevan;
'Twas at the dance—now, pause and mind,
    What care, with sorrow, shame, and sin, does,—
The feet were going like the wind,
    For they were dancing " Smash the windows".

IV.

He saw me, but he took no note,—
    He knew me not, so changed and worn;
The song I sung swelled in my throat—
    'Twas worse than all that I had borne!
I stopped, I gazed upon them there,
    I thought of happy hopes departed,
Then turned, and tottered thro' the Fair,
    And left the place all broken-hearted!

V.

Now wrap me in my old gray cloak,
    And lay me by this path-side fountain:
I think on those whose hearts I broke,
    Far, far away by Barna's mountain;
Long calm they lie where Barna's stream
    Around the churchyard wall is flowing,—
Oh! on their death-bed did they dream
    Of her that's now so quickly going?

VI.

I fear their bones in earth would stir
    With grief, were their cold earth laid o'er me,
Yet still I long to lie near her,
    The mother dear, that nursed and bore me.

I ask it with my latest breath,
　　You wont refuse your Maureen Grady—
Oh! take me, lay me near in death,
　　Near those I kilt, my Rovin' Thady!

ROMANCE OF THE BLACK ROBBER.*

I.

By a Mumhan mountain airy and stern,
A well lies circled by rock and fern,
And fiercely over a precipice near
Rusheth a waterfall brown and clear.

II.

In a hollow rent by that bright well's foam
A mighty robber once made his home,—
A man he was full sullen and dark
As ever brooded on murder stark,—

III.

A mighty man of a fearful name,
Who took their treasures from all who came,
Who hated mankind, who murdered for greed,
With an iron heart for each bloody deed.

IV.

As he sat by the torrent ford one day,
A wierd-like beldame came down the way:
Red was her mantle, and rich and fine,
But toil and travel had dimmed its shine.

V.

A war axe in his red hand he took,
And he killed the beldame beside the brook,

---

* Partly from one of the ancient Fenian romances.

And when on the greensward in death she rolled,
In her arms, lo! a babe, clad in pearls and gold!

VI.

He buried the beldame beside the wave,
And he took the child to his mountain cave,
And the first jewel his red hand met,
A Fern and a Hound on its gem were set!

VII.

Yet darkly he raised his hand to kill,
But his fierce heart smote him such blood to spill;
Oh! the rage for murder was there delayed
By the innocent smile of that infant maid!

VIII.

He made it a bed of the fern leaves green,
And he nursed it well from that evening sheen,
And day by day, as the sweet child grew,
The heart of the Robber grew softer too.

IX.

Ten long years were past and gone,
And the Robber sat by the ford's gray stone,
And there on the eve of a spring-tide day
A lordly pageant came down the way.

X.

Before them a banner of green and gold,
With a Fern and a Hound on its glittering fold,
Behind it a prince with a sad pale face,—
A mighty prince of a mighty race.

XI.

The Robber looked on the Fern and Hound,
Then sprang toward the Prince with an eager bound,
And "Why art thou sad, O king?" said he,
In the midst of that lordly companie!

XII.

His kindly purpose they all mistook,
For, though wan and worn, yet fierce his look,
And sudden a noble drew out his glaive,
And cleft his skull on the beldame's grave!

XIII.

" Sad", said the pale Prince, " my fate has been,
Since the dark enchanters have ta'en my queen,
Since they bore my child from the nurse's hand,
And keep her alway in th' enchanted land!"

XIV.

The dying robber half rose by the wave,
"Oh! enter", he cried, " you lonely cave!"
They entered,—the pale Prince found his child,
And all was joy in that mountain wild!

THE SIEGE OF CLONMEL.

A.D. 1650.

I.

I stood beside a gun upon the Western Gate
At the rising of the sun, the battle to await:
In the morning's ruddy glow showed the fires' destroying tracks,
My brave comrades all below, with their harness on their backs.

II.

Each with harness on his back, by rampart, street, and tower,
To repel the fierce attack in the sultry noontide hour;

Glittered lance and flashed the glaive, till the work of death begun;
And one cheer my comrades gave, as the ruthless foe came on!

III.

As the wild waves dash and vault 'gainst the cliffs of high Dunmore,
Fierce they mounted to th' assault, up the breach, in sweat and gore;—
As the billows backward flow at the ebbing of the main,
Back we drove the daring foe to his camp trench once again!

IV.

Out burst each roaring gun, with its mouth of hissing flame,
From its war-cloud thick and dun, as again the foemen came
For vengeance burning hot; but once more we mowed them down
With spear, and sword, and shot, 'till we drove them from the town.

V.

Cromwell kept the northern height;—as a spectre pale was he,
When he saw his men of might twice before my comrades flee;
And he pointed with his sword where the red breach smoking lay—
"Go! take it, and the Lord shall be on our side to-day!"

VI.

With psalm and trumpet swell came they on at his behest;—
Then we rammed each cannon well, and we nerved each gallant breast!

And the bloody breach we manned with fearless
    hearts and high,
The onset to withstand, or for homes and altars die!

VII.

Tottered mansion, tower, and wall at the thundering
    fire we gave;—
But thro' blood, and smoke, and all, came they on by
    dint of glaive;
'Till with wild and deafening din, fierce, to gorge
    their hate accurst,
O'er the gory breach, and in, in one destroying wave
    they burst!

VIII.

Breast to breast their charge we met with the battle's
    rage and hate,
Hand to hand, unconquered yet, with the foe we
    tried our fate.—
They were many, we were few; they were brave and
    stalworth men,
But we charged, and charged anew—'till we broke
    their ranks again!

IX.

How we cleared each narrow street when the foe-
    men's flight began!—
How we rushed on their retreat!—how we slew them
    as they ran!—
How we quaffed the wine so bright when our bloody
    task was o'er,
To the men who 'scaped the fight, and the brave who
    slept in gore!

X.

Evening's cloud came o'er the hill—darker clouds on
    Cromwell's face,
When, with all his force and skill, he could not storm
    the place!—

But our powder all was gone, and our cannon useless
    lay,
And what man could do was done, so we might no
    longer stay.

XI.

We buried those who fell, with the silence of the
    tomb,
And we left thee, brave Clonmel, 'neath the mid-
    night's friendly gloom:—
With slow and measured tread, o'er the low Bridge
    of the Dane,
And that dark breach where we bled, did we ne'er
    behold again!

THE TWO GALLOGLACHS.

I.

"I look across the moorlands drear,
    To see my Donall coming o'er:
He left me for the wars last year,
And night and day I think and fear
    I'll never, never see him more.
    Perchance he's slumbering in his gore!
Killemree! oh, Killemree!
    My days are dark, my heart is sore,
To think upon thy lovely lea
    I'll never, never see him more!

II.

Up toward the black, black north he rode,
    To fight the valiant Norman men;
His light plume in the breezes flowed,
And gallantly his armour glowed,
    As he sped down our native glen—
    I'll never see my love again;

Killemree! oh, Killemree!
  My heart is sore with sorrow, when
I think upon thy sunny lea,—
  I'll never see my love again!"

III.

Beneath a tree sat comrades two,
  Two Galloglachs in their bright mail,
All day they'd rode the foray thro'—
Wild Diarmid Keal and Donall Dhu—
  Against the Normans of the Pale.
  Said Donall of the Gilded Mail:
" Killemree! oh, Killemree!
  What dost thou fight for, Diarmid Keal?"
" I fight all for my fair countrie,
  Tall Donall of the Gilded Mail!"

IV.

" And I fight for my fair countrie,
  But eke for love I draw the brand:
To purchase fame for her and me,
My Mora of the southern lea,
  I've ever worked with heart and hand—
  I fight for love and native land,
Killemree! oh, Killemree!
  If one will fall, sure one will stand!"
Said Donall Dhu all pleasantly,
  As they sat by the Liffey strand.

V.

At blink of morn upon the dell
  The valiant Normans they descried,
Then there was groan and battle-yell;
But ere the noon brave Diarmid fell
  His comrade's rushing steed beside;
  All for his native land he died.

Killemree! oh, Killemree!
   It was a death of fame and pride,
And his was fame, the bold and free
   Who fell upon the Liffey side.

VI.

And black the oath tall Donall swore—
   "I'll have revenge for him that's slain!"
Then thro' the Norman ranks he tore,
But in their flight along the shore,
   Deep wounded, he was prisoner ta'en;
   But ere the morn he broke their chain,
Killemree! oh, Killemree!
   And bore him towards his native plain,
Resolved to die, or to be free,
   And see his true love once again!

VII.

He climbed the mountain hoar and bare,
   And darted up the highland pass:
Three foemen stood against him there—
His keen sword whirling in the air,
   He stretched the foremost on the grass;
   He clove through shield of hide and brass,
Killemree! oh, Killemree!
   The next, and from a gray rock's mass
He hurled the last right furiously,
   And 'scaped from death in that wild pass!

VIII.

As by a Norman bridge he came,
   The warder laid his lance full low,
To ask his purport and his name,—
Tall Donall's sword went down like flame,
   And cleft the warder at a blow;
   But little food and much of woe,

Killemree ! oh, Killemree !
   Until he reached her faint and slow,
And clasped young Mora tenderly,
   Thus 'scaped from bond and brand of foe !

IX.

Each day she nursed him tenderly,
   Her Donall of the Gilded Mail,
'Twas love for her that set him free,
That bore him up in far countree,
   Else he had died like Diarmid Keal.
'Twas all of joy and none of bale,
Killemree ! oh, Killemree !
   Within their native southern vale,
At bridal of that maiden free,
   And Donall of the Gilded Mail.

THE FAIRY MILL.

I.

Away to Ounanar's glancing tide,
   Where the redbreast sings on the hawthorn spray,
O'er craggy hill and moorland wide,
   The wanderer takes his lonely way.
He is a warrior young and bold,
   His path from the revel wild pursuing,
And he sits where down in Glenanar's wold*
   The ring-doves mid the dells are cooing.

II.

It is by the Pool of the Fairy Mill,
   Where the redbreast sings on the hawthorn spray,
Where heard, but unseen, in the evening still,
   Ceaseless the merry wheel worketh away ;

---

* Glenanar, a beautiful and romantic valley on the Limerick border, between Doneraile and Kilfinane.

And he lists to its plashing, wierd-like sound,
    And he drinks, by all fairy spells undaunted,
Of the crystal wave from his helmet round,
    To the Maid who dwells in that mill enchanted.

III.

He looks around in the sunset light,
    Where the redbreast sings on the hawthorn spray,
And he is aware of a maiden bright,
    Close at his side by the rock-wall gray;
Darts clear light from her star-bright eyes,
    Sweet is her love-lit smile and tender,
And her shining hair o'er her shoulders lies,
    Yellow and sheen in the sunset splendour!

IV.

"Thou hast drunk", she cries, "to the fairy maid,
    Where the redbreast sings on the hawthorn spray:
Wear in thy plume this small hair braid,
    And think on me at each close of day!"
She has placed the braid in his nodding plume;
    She's gone, like sweet Hope from a hall of mourning,
And he hears no sound save the ceaseless hum,
    And the plash of the fairy mill-wheel turning!

V.

He hies away from that haunted glen,
    Where the redbreast sings on the hawthorn spray;
But spell-bound, amid the ways of men,
    He thinks on the maid of the mill alway;
He thinks till his heart is filled with love,
    And that heart ne'er resteth, so fondly laden,
'Till he stands once more in Glenanar's grove,
    And eager calls on the fairy maiden.

VI.

He looks around in the sunset light,
  Where the redbreast sings on the hawthorn spray,
And he is aware of that maiden bright
  Close at his side by the rock-wall gray:
" To thee", he cries, " my love, I've come
  By forest green and by mountain hoary;
For thee I leave my own loved home,
  The joys of peace and the battle's glory!

VII.

Then let me live, fair maid, with thee,
  Where the redbreast sings on the hawthorn spray,
Where the fairy mill sounds merrily,
  And love shall lighten our home alway!"
Oh! her beaming smile, oh! her looks of love,
  As she leads him down by that haunted river,
And there mid Glenanar's flowery grove
  They live in cloudless joy for ever!

DUNLEVY.

I.

Dunlevy stands lone in the forest,
  To list to the bells' merry peal,
And their sounds make his young heart the sorest
  That e'er throbbed 'neath corselet of steel;
For they ring the gay bridal of Alice,
  The lady he loved long and pure,
False to him in her sire's feudal palace
  By the sweet lovely banks of the Suir.

II.

The Baron, his high Norman neighbour,
    The fond, happy bridegroom is he,
And Dunlevy's right hand's on his sabre,
    To think that such falseness could be;
For the lady had vowed o'er and over
    That nought could her fondness allure
From Dunlevy, her brave knightly lover,
    By the sweet lovely banks of the Suir.

III.

The hot noon came burning and shining
    O'er hill-top and valley and tower;
Yet still stood Dunlevy repining,
    Dark and lone in that gay wildwood bower,
Till he saw far away brightly gleaming
    Casque and spear over mountain and moor,
Till a trumpet blast startled his dreaming
    By the sweet lovely banks of the Suir.

IV.

Sudden heard he a trembling and sighing,
    And a-nigh stood his love sorrow-worn,
From her father's gay hall after flying
    Ere the bridal could bind her that morn;
And sudden away they are sweeping
    On his wild steed towards gray Craganure,
Where his bright native torrents are leaping,
    Far away from the banks of the Suir.

V.

From the gray hill that tow'rs o'er the valley
    The bridegroom and father look down,
Where the mailed knights and vassals out sally,
    All searching thro' green dale and town;

But Dunlevy from stern sire and vassal
  With his bright blooming love's now secure,
Far away in his own native castle
  From the sweet lovely banks of the Suir!

THE BATTLE OF KNOCKINOSS.

Scene: A camp-fire by the Shannon.—An old Rapparee who had served in the wars of 1641, relating the battle to his comrades.

I.

Attend, ye valiant horsemen and each bold Rapparee,
And by our blazing camp-fire a tale I'll tell to ye:—
With Murrogh's* savage army one valley's breadth away,
One noon of bleak November on Knock'noss hill we lay.

II.

Lord Taaffe was our commander, and brave Mac Alisdrum,
And 'cross the lowland meadows we saw the foeman come;
Then up spake bold Mac Alisdrum, "Now leave their wing to me";
And soon we crossed our sabres with their artillery.

---

* *Murrogh an Theothaun*, or Murrogh the Burner. He was Baron of Inchiquin, and his name is yet remembered among the peasantry as the most ferocious and bloodthirsty of Cromwell's generals.

III.

We swept them down the hill-sides, and took both
    flag and gun,
And back across the meadows we made them quickly
    run;
But swift as they retreated, more fast behind we
    bore,
Until we steeped our sabres from point to hilt in
    gore.

IV.

Alas, alas for cowards, and ho! for dauntless men!
Without one cause for flying, Lord Taaffe fled thro'
    the glen,
And all our army with him in panic rushed away,
And left us sore surrounded on Knock'noss hill that
    day.

V.

Then up spoke our commander, the brave Mac
    Alisdrum,—
"The foe pursues our comrades, this way his horse-
    men come;
Then out with each good claymore, and strike like
    brave men still!"
And at his words the foemen came charging o'er the
    hill!

VI.

Mo brón! Mo brón! the slaughter, when we mixed
    horse and man!
Loud crashed the roaring battle, like floods the red
    blood ran;
And few the foemen left us to fight another fray,
And Alisdrum they murdered at Knockinoss that
    day!

VII.

My curse upon all cowards, and ho! for brave men still!—
Long, long their bones were bleaching upon that blood-stained hill!
Then choose a good commander to lead ye to the fray,
And shun what lost the battle on Knock'noss hill that day!

THE WHITE LADYE.

I.

The Baron of Brugh* took his steel-gray steed,
    And faced the mid-day sun,
And he'd gained Glennavh,† so wild his speed,
    Ere the noontide course was run.

II.

He rode by Glennavh and by many a grave,
    O'er that lone glen's sacred rill,
And he stopped not, nor stayed, till he reached the green glade,
    By the Red Rath of the Hill.

III.

Sitting by the lone Red Rath,
    A charger's tramp heard he,
And riding nigh in the woodland path,
    Soon came the White Ladye.

---

* Brugh, in the old Irish, means a house—a large dwelling place. It is the ancient name of Bruff in the county Limerick.

† Glennavh—the Holy Glen—lies near the ancient and picturesque churchyard of Ardpatrick, about two miles west of Kilfinane. Raheen Ruadh—the Little Red Rath—lies near Cloghanathboy Castle, the beautiful seat of Lord and Lady Ashtown, a few miles south-west of Kilfinane.

IV.

She was no fairy of the place,
　　Though she shamed the fairies' speed :
Milk-white her dress, pale, pale her face,
　　And snow-white was her steed !

V.

The Baron leaped as a knight should leap,
　　All in mail, to his saddle-tree,
And away, away thro' the woods did sweep
　　After the White Ladye.

VI.

'Till deep in the lonely Gap of the Blast
　　She turned her steed around,
And charged the Baron all furious and fast,
　　As he went with a headlong bound.

VII.

A bright, bright glaive in her hand she bore,
　　And she came like a knightly foe,
And the Baron she struck on the helmet so sore,
　　That he bent to his saddle bow !

VIII.

There came a rock in his charger's path,
　　As that furious course he ran,
And with headlond plunge and with kindled wrath
　　To the ground went horse and man !

IX.

Never he rose from the rocky ground
　　'Till the sunset o'er him shone,
Then he leapt on his steed, and he looked around,
　　But the White Ladye was gone.

X.

Ere waned the next moon's silver light
    He sought that place again,
And there he saw a sad, sad sight
    All in the hollow glen.

XI.

There lay a dead knight in his path,
    Cloven from crown to crest,
And the White Ladye by the lone Red Rath
    With an arrow in her breast!

XII.

And over the Ladye the Baron stood,
    As her life began to fail,
And ever as flowed the red, red blood,
    She told her woeful tale.

XIII.

My father lived where yon gray tower
    Frowns o'er the Champion's stream;
There fled my days since childhood's hour,
    All like a pleasant dream.

XIV.

This bridal dress, with my life-blood red,
    One lovely morn I wore,
For I in gladness was to wed
    The Master of Kilmore.

XV.

The feast was spread, when in there sped
    The wild young lord of Crom,
And his spearmen tall crowded porch and hall,
    And he said for the bride he'd come!

XVI.

Up vassal sprang, and knightly guest,
    Each answering with a blow;
And soon was changed our bridal feast
    To a scene of blood and woe.

XVII.

I saw my father falling there,
    And my love lie in his gore,
And in wild despair, I knew not where,
    I fled thro' the wicket door.

XVIII.

Soon, soon I found my courser white,
    And rushed o'er vale and lea,
But ever still, since that fatal night,
    Crom's false lord follows me.

XIX.

He chased me all this fatal morn,
    He sent this arrow keen;
But never more to the battle borne,
    Shall his proud crest be seen.

XX.

For ere I fell in this lonely dell,
    My steed leapt forth amain,
And with this good sword of my dead young lord
    I cleft thro' the false knight's brain.

XXI.

Soon the Ladye died, and the Baron of Brugh
    Was a woeful wight that hour,
For the slaughtered man was his brother Hugh,
    The bold knight of Crom's dark tower!

XXII.

And ever since in the lonely night,
   And the twilight calm and still,
Glides that Ladye's sprite on her palfrey white
   By the Red Rath of the Hill!

THE BATTLE OF KILTILI.
A.D. 1599.

I.

The mountains of Limerick frown down on a plain
That laughs all in light to their summits again,
With its towers and its lakes and its rivers of song,
And its huge race of peasants so hardy and strong.

II.

Oh! hardy its peasants, and comely and tall,
But their spirits are broken, their minds are in thrall:
So, strike we a lilt of the chivalric day
When their sires swept the foe o'er these mountains away.

III.

To harry rich Coonagh fierce Norris came down
From the towers of Kilmallock, by forest and town,
Swearing castle and homestead and temple to sack,
And, O God! what a desert he left in his track!

IV.

The sun of the morning all cheerily smiled
On his ranks by Cnock Ruadh and by Coola the wild,
And how bright gleamed their spears by the tents white and fair,
As they marshalled, to plunder the green valleys there!

V.

They looked to the east and they looked to the west,
And they saw where their booty lay fairest and best;
Then they moved like a thick cloud of thunder and gloom
When it rolls o'er the plain from the crags of Sliav Bloom.

VI.

But see, they are halting! what wild music swells
By the founts of Commogue, through the forest's green dells?
'Tis the music of Eire—the fierce fiery strain
Which ne'er called her sons to the combat in vain.

VII.

"By Saint George!" says fierce Norris, and stops in his course
With his long lance stretched forth o'er the crest of his horse—
"By Saint George, 'tis the Gael! 'tis his pibroch's wild breath;
But he meets at Kilteely his masters and death!"

VIII.

'Twas the Gael. Slow they wound round the foot of Cnock Rue:
Small, small were their numbers, but steady and true;
And they saw not the foe where exulting he stood,
Till they reached the green glades from their path in the wood.

IX.

Then changed was their bearing—man closing on man,
With De Burgo their chieftain so proud in the van;
With hate in each eye, and defiance in all,
And their deep muttered war-word, "We conquer or fall".

X.

"By the turrets of Limerick!" De Burgo exclaims,
"Black Norris a meed for his ravaging claims;
Be they countless as hail-drops, we never shall go,
Till we measure our pikes with the steel of the foe".

XI.

Have ye seen Avondhu, how he rushes and fills,
When the floodgates of autumn are loosed on the hills?
So, the tall men of Limerick sweep down on the spears
Of Norris the proud and his fair cavaliers!

XII.

O Heaven! 'tis a fair sight to see how each file
Of the fierce foe is swept into carnage the while—
Sweet music to hear over forest and vale
The wild shout of triumph ring up from the Gael.

XIII.

Young Burgo is there in his trappings so bright,
And he follows his chieftain for aye through the fight;
But now he forsakes him, and cleaves his red way
Where the banner of England stands proud in the ray.

XIV.

There Norris receives him with taunt and with sneer,
With his arquebus ball and a lunge of his spear;
But the pike of young Burgo tears fierce through his head,
And he sinks by his banner 'mid piles of the dead.

XV.

On passed the young warrior unscathed by all,
The rush of his foemen, the spear-thrust and ball;
With haughtiest bearing he treads o'er the slain,
And clears a good road to his chieftain again.

XVI.

And wild cry the Saxons! Their chief, where is he?
Struck down at the foot of his own banner-tree,
And the banner is gone—there is fear on each brow,
And a wild panic spreads through their broken ranks now!

XVII.

And soon they are scattered away through the woods,
Like the grey Connacht sands by the westerly floods,
But they bear their gashed chieftain afar as they fly,
And they lay him in Mallow to rave and to die.

XVIII.

And the dreams of his murders came over him there
With the shadow of death and the doom of despair,
And the sun had scarce travelled ten times through the blue
Ere he slept his last sleep by the swift Avondhu.

XIX.

Thus fought the huge men of the plain long ago,
Thus chased they from Limerick the hard-hearted
    foe—
May we never meet death till we see them again
Striking up for old Eire as fearless as then!

ROMANCE OF THE FAIRY WAND.

I.

'Mid Gailty's woody highlands, by a torrent's lonely
    shore,
There dwelt a banished monarch in the dusky days
    of yore;
Long the pleasant Munster valleys had own'd his
    kingly sway,
'Till rose a fierce usurper, and reft his throne away.

II.

No vassals filled his chambers, no courtiers thronged
    his hall;
His bright-eyed little daughter and a gray-haired
    chief were all—
Were all the friends that never would forsake him
    in his woe,
When he fled, a careworn exile, to that tower in
    Aherloe.

III.

Around that highland castle, by the shady forest
    springs,
With a heart for ever dreaming of all bright and
    lovely things,

Roamed that regal little maiden every golden summer e'en,
Watched and loved, where'er she wandered, by the radiant Fairy Queen.

IV.

The sunset light was reddening on the crest of tall Bein Gar,*
As lay that little maiden 'neath the flowery woods afar;—
"Spreads this land", she said, "how lovely 'neath the purple sunset's light,
But Hy Ganra's bard has told me of a world more fair and bright!

V.

Through that land I'd wish to wander; there I'd ask a warrior train
Of its queen, to set my father on his Munster throne again".
Oh! the words she scarce had uttered, when there shone a radiance sheen,
Up and down the shady valley, and the forest depths between!

---

* *Bein Gar*—the sharp summit—the name by which Gailty Mor is principally known among the peasantry. The castle of Dun Grod—the one mentioned in the ballad—lies on the side of a glen to the westward of Bein Gar, and is one of the most ancient buildings of that description in Ireland. *Tir-n-an-Oye*, the Land of Perpetual Youth, was the Heaven of the ancient inhabitants of Ireland. The great Mitchelstown cavern, at the back of the Gailty mountains, is said by the peasantry to be one of the entrances to Tir-n-an-Oge. They say that, should a person cross the stream at the far end of the cavern, he could never by his own power return —that he should become an inhabitant of Fairyland for ever after.

VI.

On the song-birds fell a silence, was no sound
    through earth or air,
'Till in robes of snowy splendour stood a Heaven-
    browed lady there;
With beaming eyes down-looking on the little maid
    stood she,
All the glad birds singing round her again from
    bower and tree!

VII.

Then spoke the Queen of Fairy with a sweet, heart-
    thrilling tone:
"Thou hast wished, oh! little dreamer, for a sight
    of our fair zone;
Then a gift of power I bring thee: take this snowy
    wand, and when
Thou dost long to see our bright land, raise it thrice
    in this wild glen".

VIII.

Scarce the witching words were spoken when the
    Fairy Queen was gone,
But a trailing light behind her down the silent val-
    leys shone;
And up stood that beauteous maiden, instant bound
    in fairy spell,
And thrice she raised the white wand in that flower-
    starred forest dell!

IX.

Sudden, sudden stood beside her a milk-white
    palfrey fleet,
And a-nigh a mounted esquire in bright mail from
    crown to feet,

Spell-bound, mounted that young maiden, and away, wild, wild away,
O'er Gailty's dreamy highlands like a flash of light went they!

X.

Sudden fled the sunset Heavens, and a mighty vault instead,
Lit with many-tinted crystals, high o'er their pathway spread;
Cavern spars gleamed all around them with the white stars' silver flame,
'Till they crossed th' Enchanted River and to Tir-n-an-Oge they came!

XI.

Oh! that land of endless joyance, oh! that world of beauty bright,
With its green and Heavenly mountains bathed all in silver light,
With its calm sky ever gleaming all in crystal sheen above,
And its plains of bright wild splendour where the happy spirits rove!

XII.

With its clear streams ever singing pleasant songs by hill and wood,
With its silent, flower-bright valleys, where the soul alone might brood
On the splendours all around it, which gray time can ne'er destroy,
And for ever, and for ever, on its own immortal joy!

XIII.

Scarce an hour unto the maiden in that land had
    passed away,
When they found a mighty falchion—beside their
    path it lay—
"Take this falchion to my father", said the maid,
    "for some sweet lore—
Some strange power doth sudden tell me 'twill
    regain his right once more".

XIV.

Sped the esquire with the falchion to the exiled
    monarch back,
And alone went forth the maiden on her silent,
    Heavenly track,
Till beside a crystal river towered a diamond palace
    sheen,
And, with all her court around her, there she found
    the Fairy Queen.

XV.

"By the magic gift you gave me,—by this wand of
    strangest power,
Send me back, oh! radiant empress, to the world
    for one short hour,—
Back to Dun Grod's hoary castle, that my father I
    may see,
And he'll leave dark woe and sorrow, and I'll bring
    him back with me".

XVI.

"Few are they", said that bright empress, "who
    would leave this land again;
Yet go! and on thy swift course thou shalt have be-
    fitting train".

Away the Munster princess and her fairy train are gone,
Through the green vales, through the cavern, through the darkness, to the sun!

XVII.

When she reached the green Earth's valleys,—oh! that wondrous fairy zone!—
'Stead of two short hours of gladness, ten long years away had flown!
In the land were many changes, 'twas the golden summer time,
And they asked a youthful peasant, "Who now reigns in this sweet clime?"

XVIII.

"Duan reigns, our aged monarch; he has slain th' usurping lord,
And regained fair Munster's valleys by the might of his good sword;
But, oh! lovely, lovely lady, are you come from Fairyland,
You look so bright and beauteous on this morning fresh and bland?"

XIX.

The lady could not answer, so filled with joy was she:
With her maids and fairy gallants sped she on o'er hill and lea,
'Till she reached her father's palace where it stood by Shannon's wave,
And joyful was the welcome that the gladsome monarch gave!

XX.

Soon he led to his bright daughter a champion young and tall,—
"This be he, whose gallant father still was faithful in my fall,
Thou canst ne'er find champion braver, thou canst ne'er find love so fond:
Wilt thou go, then, as thou sayest—wilt thou raise the fairy wand?"

XXI.

She looked on that young champion and at her fairy train,
Gave the wand, and never turned her unto Tir-n-an-Oge again.
Oh! merry was the bridal, and as glad the reigning time,
Of that princess and her champion o'er the pleasant Munster clime!

THE TEMPLAR KNIGHT.

Mid Corrin's haunted wildwoods, where the summer winds are straying,
  Around a glade of brightness, from dells and leafy bowers,
There stands a steed caparisoned, a small steed wildly neighing
  To a boy and fair girl playing by Glendinan's high towers;*

---

* Glendinan, an extensive valley at the north side of the Bally-Houra mountains, facing the plain of Limerick. At its upper extremity lies a small, oblong, and dilapidated stone chamber, like a grave, called by the country people

And gaily round them winging, the merry birds are
    singing,
    And the stream its waves is flinging with a glad
        voice mid the flowers.

II.

Moves the steed with sportful neighings, near and
    nearer to his master,
    With axe and spear crossed bravely on his gilded
        saddle-tree,
Where springs the boy with shout of joy, and, than
    the fleet winds faster,
    His comrade, spurs he past her, with a bearing
        bold and free;
Then sudden cries: "Ho, yonder! see the magic
    halls of wonder,
    Where the wizard old doth ponder on his spells
        to fetter me!"

III.

Like a knight of peerless valour on his wild steed he
    is sweeping,
    Toward the wizard tower he fancies in the dreamy
        forest shade,—
With lance in rest for foeman's breast, his magic foe
    unsleeping,
    In swift course he is keeping across that sunlit
        glade!
And thus each evening golden, mid those mossy
    wild-woods olden,
    By dark care unbeholden, lived that boy and
        bright-eyed maid.

Iscur's Bed; about a mile below which, on the edge of a glen, are the remains of an old building, which, according to tradition, was an establishment of the Knights Templars.

IV.

Years have passed—bright years of gladness—and
   their bridal bells are ringing
  Along the summer mountains from that forest
   wild and wide;
Ah! thus from early childhood in the heart should
   love be springing,
  Soul to soul in fondness clinging from its golden
   morning tide;
Yet, alas! for Gerald's dreaming of a bride in
   beauty beaming,
  Mora's gone ere morn's first gleaming—falsely
   fled from Corrin side!

V.

As he waited by the altar, fair and fond the dreams
   that bound him,—
  Chief of Houra's sunny green-woods, with a bride
   as fair as May,—
And his look was calmly joyous to the vassals
   circled round him,
  Till the tale of sorrow found him that his bride
   had fled away,—
His love, his anger scorning, a stranger's home
   adorning,
  To Carrignour that morning with its baron bold
   and gay.

VI.

The priest hath words of comfort, the mother
   mournful sighing,
  The vassals' shouts of fury loud as battle trumpets blown,
And, "Bring me", cries young Gerald, "my war-
   steed, that out-flying,

Ere the purple day be dying, ere her paramour be
    flown,—
That the traitor lord may learn my vengeance red
    and stern,
    Ere he treads his native fern by the Funcheon's
        valleys lone!"

VII.

He has donned his battle harness, and away so wild
    careering,
    His good steed bears him bravely towards the
        valleys of Glenroe,
Till in the golden noontide, from a forest hill down
    peering,
    Little caring, little fearing, so he meet his traitor
        foe,
Where a stream its tide is sending in many a silver
    bending,
    He espies the false pair wending through the
        flowery dells below.

VIII.

By the baron kneels the maid at the evening's calm
    returning,
    But love is drowned in sorrow, and joy is changed
        to fear,—
By the baron kneels the maid all alone and wildly
    mourning,
    And his tales with warm love burning she never
        more shall hear;
For away young Gerald straineth from the spot
    where she remaineth,
    And the baron's life-blood staineth his conquering
        border spear!

IX.

But revenge ne'er changed the bosom from its dark and dreary madness
   To joy, and thus with Gerald as he rides o'er moor and moss,—
"Ah! the shadow of despair", he cries, "has sunk my hope in sadness,
   Love's gold I sought in gladness, and find it leaden dross;
So away from lovely Mulla, where she sings by height and hollow,
   Another path I'll follow,—a champion of the cross!"

X.

It was a golden morning mid summer's reign of splendour,
   Young Gerald took his lance and steed, and sped from Houra's wold;
But the fond farewell, when with sweet spell immortal love doth lend her
   Words mournful true and tender, no weeping maiden told,
Yet one true heart weepeth ever since he left his native river,
   And no joy the world can give her, his mother sad and old.

XI.

And she cries: "Again, oh! never shall I see my Gerald riding
   To the chase in merry greenwood at the blithesome peep of morn,
Shall his looks of gladness cheer me, shall his words of love come gliding,
   With peace and joy abiding, to my heart so sorrow-torn!"

But with time, despair retreating, hope springeth up
  unfleeting,
  Else her heart had ceased its beating,—she had
  died in grief forlorn.

XII.

Long she hoped for his returning to his hall with
  name of glory,
  Till the flowers of ten bright summers lay dead on
  mead and tomb ;
Then unseen he stood one morning on Corrin's sum-
  mit hoary,
  Gazing round that land of story on each well-known
  scene of bloom ;—
Dreams of fair maids he was spurning, who might
  come with warm love burning,
  When they heard of his returning, for he wore the
  Templar plume !

XIII.

Many dreams of his sweet childhood there his memory
  might borrow,
  Yet he entered with a sinking heart his native hall
  once more.
There he found his mother sitting in her lorn and
  silent sorrow,
  As she sat that golden morrow when he left his
  home of yore ;—
Glad and sudden up she started, "Oh! we'll never
  more be parted!"
  And she died all joyous-hearted in his arms by
  Mulla's shore !

XIV.

To Glendinan Sir Gerald has brought across the
  ocean
  Five Templars, he their leader, with all their vassal power,

And thrice each day out ringing with a sad and
  solemn motion,
 Tolls their bell to meet devotion o'er cot and hall
   and bower:
And long their banner knightly in the sunshine glit-
  tered brightly,
 To the breezes fluttered lightly from that ancient
   Templar tower!

ROMANCE OF THE STONE COFFIN.

I.

Mournfully, sing mournfully
 The hollow cave of green Cnoc-Brōn,*
It faceth to the golden west
 'Mid the steep mountain's ridge of stone,
 Boulder and crag around it strown,
  Its entrance from the wild wind save,—
Mournfully, sing mournfully
 The maiden of that lonely cave;
 The brightest, fairest maid was she
  From dark Sliav Bluim to Cleena's wave.†

---

* *Cnoc Brōn*, the Hill of Sorrow. It is situated about two miles north of Kildorrery, on the confines of the County Cork. Between it and Cnoc Aodh, another steep mountain, there is a narrow and deep pass, called Barna Dearg—the Red or Bloody Gap,—in consequence of the numerous battles fought there in ancient ages. Cnoc Brōn is supposed to be the ancient Sliabh Caoin, or the Hill of Lamentation, where Mahon, a Munster prince, was murdered in the tenth century. In a ridge of rocks which runs towards the summit of the hill lies a small cave, called by the peasantry *Shaumer an Nora*, or Nora's Chamber. In this cave, according to tradition, a young woman, named Nora, hollowed out her coffin, and died as told in the ballad.

† That part of the ocean round the coast of Cork is called in Irish poetry the "Waters of Cleena".

II.

Mournfully, sing mournfully,
  In gray Kilmallock stands a tower,
And there her lordly father dwelt,
  Long, long ago, in pride and power;
  Oh! ample was bright Norah's dower,
    And many suitors round her came:
But mournfully, sing mournfully,
    An old, proud chieftain owned his flame,
A false and gloomy man was he,
    Yet high he stood in martial fame.

III.

Mournfully, sing mournfully,
  Some curse was on her father then,
He would not list to her true love
  For young Sir Redmond of the Glen;
  They forced her to the shrine, and when
    Within its sacred bound they stayed,
Mournfully, sing mournfully,
    The withered bride-groom, that fair maid,
You ne'er have seen, and ne'er shall see,
    A bridal match so ill arrayed.

IV.

Mournfully, sing mournfully,
  As died the sunset golden red,
The bridegroom told, to pay her scorn,
  His own dear lady was not dead!
  Alas! 'twas truth the old man said,
    Then Nora started from her rest;
And mournfully, sing mournfully,
    She plunged a dagger in his breast,
And fled by glen and bower and tree,
    Until she reached Cnoc Brūn's wild crest!

V.

Mournfully, sing mournfully,
  Her madness, and her guilt, and pain,
As fled that fatal summer night,
  And morn leapt o'er the hills again;
  Oh! tears may gush like autumn rain,
    Yet the heart's sorrow will not go;
And mournfully, sing mournfully,
  Young Nora's guilt, and pain, and woe
From her poor bosom would not flee,
  Howe'er her tears might fall or flow.

VI.

Mournfully, sing mournfully,
  The fruits and wild herbs of the fell
Were her sole food for many a day,
  Her drink a lone and rock-bound well;
  At length she prayed, and who can tell
    But God did hear her woful prayer,
That mournfully, oh! mournfully,
  She'd die on that wild mountain there,
And leave, for Heaven, her misery,
  Her guilt, her madness, and despair.

VII.

Mournfully, sing mournfully,
  As by the cave one noon she sate,
Far looking towards her father's hall,
  Still as the crags and desolate,
  She saw in burnished harness plate
    Many a fiercer charger spurn the grass,
And mournfully, sing mournfully,
  Two armies, each in one bright mass,
Rush into battle thunderingly
  Beneath her in the Bloody Pass!

VIII.

Mournfully, sing mournfully,
  She knew one tall and fatal spear—
'Twas young Sir Redmond of the Glen,
  Forth rushing in his wild career,
  And there the foe's red banner near,
    Where knight and kern lay strewn and killed,
Mournfully, sing mournfully,
    Her brave young lover's blood was spilled,
And there that hapless hour sat she,
    The measure of her sorrows filled!

IX.

Mournfully, sing mournfully,
  She took the huge dirk which had slain
That old and false and villain chief,
  Red crusted with its bloody stain;
  A time-worn crumbling stone had lain
    Beside the cave for many a year,
Oh! mournfully, sing mournfully,
    "Of this", she cried, "I'll make my bier,
And die where o'er my misery
    No human eye can shed a tear!"

X.

Mournfully, sing mournfully,
  Night and morn and sunset red,
The lady plied that dagger strong,
  'Till she had scooped her narrow bed.
  Now the sweet summer time was fled,
    And all its flow'rs decayed and gone;
And mournfully, sing mournfully,
    Weak and worn, and sad and wan,
There on an autumn eve sat she,
    The last that o'er her misery shone.

XI.

Mournfully, sing mournfully,
    She laid her on her bier of stone,
And there and then in that wild cave,
    She died for love all, all alone;
    There mid the ridge of stern Cnoc Brōn,
    The peasants found her lifeless clay,
And mournfully, oh! mournfully,
    They bare her to the abbey gray,
Where sleeps she lowly, silently,
    Within her coffin stone alway.

ROMANCE OF THE BANNER.*

I.

There was a banner old, in a tower by th' ocean bound,
Its device a boat of gold, a lady, and a hound;
Then, gentles, sit around, and a tale I'll tell to ye,
All about the old green banner of that tower by Cleena's sea.

II.

"Where away, oh! where away?" asked the hoary marinere,
From a rock that towered so gray o'er the waters broad and clear—
"To seek my true love dear, doth he live, or is he dead!"
Cried young Marron, with her wolf-hound, as o'er the waves she sped.

---

* An episode in a Fenian romance.

III.

Night, with her starry train, o'er the hound and fair ladye—
Rose the shark from out the main, stealing slowly on their lee,
On them dark and wild looked he,—gazed the wolf-hound fierce on him,
While he plunged and glared and passed them in the ghostly midnight dim!

IV.

Vanished the starlight pale, came rosy morn once more,
As that boat so small and frail sped the purpling billows o'er,
A tall coast towered before, with great, blue hills behind,
And "Perchance", cried Marron, weeping, "here my true love I may find!"

V.

The sharp keel grates the sand;—ah! the sight before her there,
Wrecks on wrecks along the strand, stark bones whitening in the air;
Down she sat in her despair. "Ah! my Turlogh brave", said she,
"The storm came down upon him, and his bones lie in the sea!"

VI.

And floating on the wave beside the sand below,
The glittering plume she gave her love two moons ago!

Oh! the madness of her woe, oh! her shriek of wild despair,
As she sank, like death had struck her, on the wet sands swooning there!

VII.

A youth with agile bound, of high and princely mien,
Welcomed by Marron's hound,—no foe to her I ween,—
Has darted from the screen of an old, deserted fane,
And o'erjoyed young Marron wakens in her Turlogh's arms again!

VIII.

Sank crew and galley trim when the wild tempest roared,
And left alive but him, to Marron thus restored;
Nought saved he but his sword from thundering blast and brine,
And he says, "We'll seek green Desmond, and thou never more shalt pine!"

IX.

On their course the night came down without one planet bright,
Great clouds of dreary brown quenched all their trembling light.
Up to the lowering height the hound his gaze has thrown,
And a sudden yell breaks from him, and a low, sad, wailing moan!

X.

Sudden the lightning's flash came darting out on high,
And the mighty thunder's crash boomed o'er the boundless sky,
And with a vengeful cry the storm began to rave,
And lowered them in the hollows, and tossed them o'er the wave.

XI.

"Oh! for the mighty rock where stands my castle gray"—
Amid the tempest's shock, thus the young chief did say:—
"My heart feels no dismay, but all for love and thee,
So soon to sink and perish beneath the roaring sea!"

XII.

Out in the rushing wind upon the greedy wave,
His arm around her twined, wildly he sprang to save;
The boat whirled stave by stave on toward the disstant shore,
And the wolf-hound plunged and turned, then dashed right on before.

XIII.

The golden morn had broke o'er sea and lovely land,
When calmly they awoke—'twas on their native strand,
They made a banner grand, and on its gleaming fold
Was the hound and lovely lady, and the boat of ruddy gold.

ROSE CONDON.

I.

Over valley and rock and lea,
    Merrily strike the wild harp's strain,—
For the fairest maid in the south countrie
    Hath come to our Funcheon's side again;
Far mid the mountains of Green Fear-muighe,*
    In lone Crag Thierna† many a day
Dwelt she long with the fairy throng,
    Mourning for her home alway.

II.

An Ardrigh's crown is yellow and bright—
    Fill the glens with the wild harp's tone—
But it may not match those locks of light
    So loosely o'er her fair brows thrown;
And the glance of her eyes, oh! mortal wight
    Never such glory saw before;
And her neck as the wild rose soft and white,
    Lone blooming by the Funcheon's shore.

III.

She is daughter of Condon brave—
    Strike the wild harp's string of pride—
The fiercest chief where thy waters rave,
    Dark Oun Mór of the rushing tide;

---

* *Fear-Muighe-Feine*—the plain of the Fenian men—which anciently included the baronies of Condon and Clongibbon, together with what is at present called the barony of *Fermoy*, is walled in on the south by the Nagles mountains, and on the north by the Gailtees and Bally-Houras, or mountains of Mole. It was called Armoy, and I believe Ardmulla, by Spenser. Along its southern side flows the Blackwater, forming a succession of the most beautiful and romantic scenes in the south of Ireland. The whole plain anciently belonged to the O'Keeffes.

† Crag Thierna, or Corrin Thierna, a romantic steep, eastward of Fermoy, and celebrated in the legends of the peasantry as one of the great fairy palaces of Munster.

Nine moons have silvered the Funcheon's wave,
  Since by the towers of strong Cloghlee
The fondness of her heart she gave
  To the banished Knight of thy woods, Gailtee!

IV.

O Love! thy power grows day by day—
  Strike the wild harp high and bold—
Three eves had purpled the mountains gray,
  And young Clongibbon had ta'en his hold,
Reta'en his hold, regained his sway,
  All for the love of Condon's child,
And chased the Saxon far away
  Beyond the pale of his mountains wild!

V.

Three eves more o'er Funcheon's tide—
  Strike the wild harp clear and sweet—
Rose Condon sat by the water side,
  Her brave, triumphant love to meet:
The sunset in his purple pride,
  Over the far-off crests of Mole,
And thro' the glens and forest wide
  A sweet and dreamy silence stole.

VI.

Long she waits her lover's tread—
  Strike the wild harp tenderly—
Till day's bright legions all are fled,
  And the white stars peer thro' the forest tree;
Ha! now he comes by the river bed,
  With his martial step and bearing high;
But why is the maiden's heart adread,
  As her warrior love draws fondly nigh?

VII.

Does victory paint a warrior's mail—
    Strike the wild harp fearfully—
With swarth gold gems and diamonds pale,
    And his plume with the sunbow's radiancy?
Her lover's armour thro' the vale
    Sheddeth a wild and elfin gleam,
And strange sounds on the breezes sail,
    Sweet echoing o'er the star-lit stream.

VIII.

The warrior now beside her stands—
    Strike the wild harp sad and low—
And takes in his her trembling hands,
    But her loved knight ne'er gazèd so!
Oh! 'twas the king of the fairy bands
    That bound her in his spells that night,
And bore her swift to the elfin lands,
    Far, far away in his love-winged flight!

IX.

From Oun Mór's tide to Carrig'nour,*—
    Strike the wild harp rushingly—
From far Mocollop's mighty tower
    To the storied hill of Kil-da-righ,
Many a man ere morning hour
    Thro' the wildwoods rode amain:
They sought the maid in hall and bower,
    But fruitless was their search and vain.

---

* Carriganour, a very ancient castle a few miles below Mitchelstown, on the banks of the Funcheon. Mocollop, a huge pile eastward of Cloghleigh, on the shore of the Blackwater. *Kil-da-righ*—the Church of the two Kings—at present Kildorrery, a small town on the Cork border, between Fermoy and Kilmallock.

X.

Condon sat within his hall—
  Strike the wild harp mournfully—
Sadness did his heart enthral,
  Grief for her he might not see;
Searching still, Clongibbon tall
  Roamed the forests lone and drear,
Like maniac man bereft of all
  The joyance of this earthly sphere.

XI.

Joy in lone Crag Thierna's steep!—
  Strike the harp o'er hill and wold—
Glad feasts the Fairy King did keep
  For young Rose with the locks of gold;
But ah! the maid did nought but weep,
  And eight bright moons had lost their flame,
Yet still by Oun Mór swift and deep,
  In sorrow she was still the same.

XII.

Nine sweet nights have robed the dells—
  Strike the wild harp bold and high—
Since out with martial trumpet swells
  The fairy throngs came trooping by;
Round lone Molaga's holy cells,*
  Beneath the midnight moon they played,
While she, the victim of their spells,
  Sat lorn within the ruin's shade.

---

* *Teompal Molaga*—the Temple or Church of Saint Molaga—an extremely beautiful and picturesque ruin, about a mile north-east of Kildorrery, on a bend of the Funcheon. Beside it is an ancient well dedicated to the saint, to which the peasantry ascribe many virtues, and of which many strange legends are told.

XIII.

It is beside a fountain fair—
    Strike the wild harp sweet and low—
With sad heart brooding on her care,
    She looks into the wave below;
A shadow glides before her there,
    And looking up, beside her stands
An aged man with snow-white hair,
    With pitying eyes and clasped hands!

XIV.

A mitre decked in golden sheen—
    Strike the wild harp wonderingly—
A vestment as the shamrock green,
    And sandals of the mountain tree
He wears: the ancient Saint, I ween!
    Ah! he hath heard the maiden's moan,
And bids her drink with brow serene,
    One pure draught from a cup of stone,

XV.

The fays may sport o'er hill and plain—
    Strike the wild harp glad and bold—
But never shall their power again
    In magic gyve that maiden hold;
One cool, bright draught she scarce had ta'en,
    Scarce looked upon the vestment cross,
When fearful died the fairy strain,
    O'er moonlit crag and lonely moss!

XVI.

Short time their splendid pageant shone—
    Strike the harp with gladsome thrill—
Then faded in the moonlight wan
    Far o'er Caher Drina's castled hill;*

---

* Caher Drian, or Fort Prospect, a castle about three miles south-east of Carriganour. *Oun-na-Geerait*—the River

Short time the moonbeams glowed upon
    The mitre and the vestment bright,
The maiden turned, the saint was gone,
    Impatient to his home of light!

XVII.

Oh! joy! she sees the eastern ray—
    Strike the wild harp glad and clear—
The herald of a golden day,
    The fairest in the circling year;
It is the first bright morn of May,
    And stream and plain smile calmly now,
And many a wild bird pours his lay,
    In gladness from the greenwood bough.

XVIII.

Oh! Freedom leadeth where she list—
    Strike the wild harp's string of pride—
Wild joy the maid can ne'er resist
    Impels towards Oun-na-Geerait's side;
There, while the stream by day is kissed,
    A strange sight meets her wandering eyes—
It is not golden morning mist
    With glad larks o'er it in the skies:

XIX.

The red fires of a Saxon raid—
    Strike the wild harp fierce and high—
With scattered smoke o'er many a glade
    Blue curling to the breezeless sky;

---

of the Champion—a tributary of the Funcheon. Glashmona, a stream rising in the Bally-Houra mountains. By the banks of this torrent, the peasantry tell many legends relating to the battles fought there between the ancient tribes. *Aha Phooka*—the Ford of the Spirit—is a steep and dangerous pass leading from the county Limerick into the Clongibbon's country.

Helmet and lance, and well-tried blade,
    Gleam brightly from the forest deep,
And many a creacht beneath the shade
    Lie silent in their morning sleep!

XX.

"Ho! wake the tired creachts from their rest!"—
    Strike the harp o'er hill and plain—
On toward Kilfinane's mountain crest
    The raiders take their course again;
Fear gathereth in the maiden's breast,
    As wind away that fierce-browed horde,
Taking their pathway to the west,
    Triumphant thro' the Spirit's Ford.

XXI.

Is that the thunder of the flood—
    Strike the harp all fiercely now—
She hears wild rising from the wood,
    And echoing up the steep hill's brow?
Oh! rushing back in panic mood,
    Like leaves before a mountain wind,
The raiders come in dust and blood,
    Her father and his clan behind!

XXII.

And who is he her sire before—
    Strike the wild harp high and grand—
Scattering the raiders evermore
    Before the wide sweep of his brand?
Ah! well within her fond heart's core
    She knows her lover's martial form,
As fiercely on the river's shore
    He sweepeth thro' the battle storm.

XXIII.

Oh, God! that lance stroke thro' his side—
    Raise the wild harp's mournful tone—

Stretches her sire where redly glide
    The swift waves o'er their bed of stone!
Down speeds the maid, whate'er betide,
    Swift as Glashmona's startled hare,
And soon—death, danger, all defied—
    She bendeth o'er her father there!

XXIV.

Oh! joy, it is no mortal wound—
    Strike the glad harp to the skies—
She lifts his faint head from the ground,
    With heaving breast and tearful eyes.
With wondering eyes he looks around,
    As wakening sense asserts its reign—
Oh! joy of joys! the lost is found
    To cheer his course thro' life again!

XXV.

The clangour of the fight is o'er—
    Strike the wild harp's proudest lay—
Few raiders from that river shore
    Passed westward thro' the Spirit's Way;
Glad was the look Clongibbon wore,
    His herds reta'en, his valleys free,
As clasped he in his arms once more
    The gold-haired maid of green Fear-Muighe!

THE BATTLE OF THURLES.
A.D. 1174.

I.

By the gray walls of Thurles in O'Fogarty's land
We came to the trysting with banner and brand:
'Twas no true-loves to meet, 'twas no fond vows to say,
But to conquer the foeman, or die in the fray.

II.

Royal Roderick was there with his bravest and best,
The wild fearless clans from the vales of the West;
Royal Donal came up from the green hills of Clare,
With his stately Dalcassians, like lions from their lair.

III.

Where our Ardrigh was resting, the sunburst gleamed wide,
Donal's three bloody lions waved proud at its side,
And *mavrone*, on that morn how we vowed and we swore
To freshen their tints in the black Norman's gore.

IV.

Out rode Earl Strongbow from Waterford gate,
With his bowmen and spearmen in armour of plate,
And they harried rich ploughland, and dungeon and hall,
To O'Fogarty's mountains from fair Carrick's wall.

V.

This news reached Marisco in strong Alia Cliath,*
And he smiled on his warriors a grim smile of glee,
And like wolves scenting carnage, with rapine and flame,
For their share in the booty to Thurles they came.

VI.

In the sun gleamed their armour, waved their flags in the gale,
Few warriors amongst us had helmet or mail:
But the hearts in our bosoms were fearless and strong, [long.
And we clove thro' their corselets and helmets ere

---

* *Baila-Aha-Cliath*—the Town of the Ford of Hurdles—Dublin.

VII.

Out rode the two kings mid our gallant array—
Small need then for words: well we knew what
    they'd say;
But they pointed their spears where they wished us
    to go,
And we rushed in their path on the iron-clad foe.

VIII.

The foe levelled lances our charge to withstand,
And thick flew their arrows as we closed hand to
    hand;
And full stoutly they stood, for brave robbers were
    they,
Who would part with their lives ere they'd part
    with their prey.

IX.

Oh! the crash of the onset as steel clanged on steel!
Oh! the *Ferrah* we gave as our blows made them
    reel!
Oh! the joy of our vengeance as onward we poured,
Till we smote them as Brian smote the fierce Danish
    horde!

X.

Earl Strongbow for life flies tow'rds Waterford Gate,
But few vassals around him his orders await;
By the brave walls of Thurles 'neath our vengeance
    they died—
Wild we feasted that night by the Suir's reddened
    tide!

ROSSNALEE.

I.

The fairy woman of the wood,
    Rossnalee! oh, Rossnalee!
Hath set the spell in her cave so rude,
And she cries, "Is't for sorrow, or all for good,
That the lovers shall meet in the secret wood,
  By the crystal waters of Rossnalee?"

II.

The fairy woman of the wood,
    Rossnalee! oh, Rossnalee!
With her crimson gown and her scarlet hood,
Cries again, "'Tis for sorrow, and nought for good,
That the lovers shall meet in the secret wood,
    By the crystal waters of Rossnalee!"

III.

Many hearts the wild wars rue,
    Rossnalee! oh, Rossnalee!
Mac Donogh's daughter weepeth too,
As she cometh to meet her lover true,
For war's sad chances well she knew,
    By the crystal waters of Rossnalee.

IV.

The first step she took from her father's door,
    Rossnalee! oh, Rossnalee!
The ban-dog howled on the barbican floor,
And her little dove cooed in the turret o'er,
With a voice of wailing and sadness sore,
    By the crystal waters of Rossnalee!

V.

The next step she took from her home so dear,
  Rossnalee! oh, Rossnalee!
She heard a low voice in her ear,
Though she saw but a white owl floating near—
"Thou'rt the sweetest blossom to grace a bier,
  By the crystal waters of Rossnalee!"

VI.

As she went down where the crags are piled,
  Rossnalee! oh, Rossnalee!
She saw a little elfish child,
And it cried with a voice all strange and wild,
"Go back! thou lady fair and mild,
  By the crystal waters of Rossnalee!"

VII.

As she crossed the rath and the war-grave rude,
  Rossnalee! oh, Rossnalee!
Cried she of the spells and the scarlet hood,*
"If thou goest, thou goest for sorrow, not good,
And the earth shall be dyed with my darling's blood,
  By the crystal waters of Rossnalee!"

VIII.

But 'gainst fair warning and friendly threat,
  Rossnalee! oh, Rossnalee!
She answers, "My heart's on the trysting set,
And how can I mourn, and how regret,
That I meet with my gallant De Barrette
  By the crystal waters of Rossnalee?"

---

* Fairies are believed by the peasantry to appear frequently in the form of an old woman clad in red garments, always with some benevolent intention.

IX.

Where the mountain ash bends over the wave,
    Rossnalee! oh, Rossnalee!
She's clasped in the arms of her lover brave,
Who cries, "Ten kisses for love I crave,
For my new-won knighthood and conquering glaive,
    By the crystal waters of Rossnalee!"

X.

"Mac Donogh, aboo!" From the darksome wood,
    Rossnalee! oh, Rossnalee!
Rushed her sire and his vassals in savage mood,—
"Ho! traitor, my vengeance this hour is good,
For thou'st won thy spurs with my best son's blood,
    By the crystal waters of Rossnalee!"

XI.

Three vassals were cloven through basnet and brain,
    Rossnalee! oh, Rossnalee!
When an arrow shot from the wood amain,
To stretch De Barrette upon the plain,
But the heart of the maiden it cleft in twain,
    By the crystal waters of Rossnalee!

XII.

Down fell the knight by his true love's side,
    Rossnalee! oh, Rossnalee!
With a wound in his breast both deep and wide,—
"Oh! death in thy arms is sweet!" he cried;
And thus these lovers so faithful died
    By the crystal waters of Rossnalee!

XIII.

De Barrette he sleeps in that lonely dell,
  Rossnalee! oh, Rossnalee!
Where like a knight in his harness he fell:
But she that he loved so true and well
Lies low in the vault of her sire's chapelle
  By the crystal waters of Rossnalee!

CROSSING THE BLACKWATER.

A.D. 1603.

I.

We stood so steady,
 All under fire,
We stood so steady,
Our long spears ready
 To vent our ire—
To dash on the Saxon,
Our mortal foe,
And lay him low
 In the bloody mire!

II.

'Twas by Blackwater,
 When snows were white,
'Twas by Blackwater,
Our foes for the slaughter
 Stood full in sight;
But we were ready
With our long spears,
And we had no fears
 But we'd win the fight.

III.

Their bullets came whistling
    Upon our rank,
Their bullets came whistling,
Their spears were bristling
    On th' other bank:
Yet we stood steady,
And each good blade,
Ere the morn did fade,
    At their life-blood drank.

IV.

"Hurra! for Freedom!"
    Came from our van,
"Hurra! for Freedom!
Our swords—we'll feed 'em
    As but we can—
With vengeance we'll feed e'm!"
Then down we crashed,
Through the wild ford dashed
    And the fray began!

V.

Horses to horses,
    And man to man—
O'er dying horses
And blood and corses
    O'Sullivan,
Our general, thundered,
And we were not slack
To slay at his back
    Till the flight began.

VI.

Oh! how we scattered
   The foemen then—
Slaughtered and scattered,
And chased and shattered,
   By shore and glen;—
To the wall of Moyallo,
Few fled that day,—
Will they bar our way
   When we come again?

VII.

Our dead freres we buried,—
   They were but few,—
Our dead freres we buried
Where the dark waves hurried
   And flashed and flew:
Oh! sweet be their slumber
Who thus have died
In the battle's tide,
   Inisfail, for you!

ROMANCE OF MEERGAL AND GARMON.

FYTTE THE FIRST.

I.

'Tis Meergal of the Mountain that sighs so mournfully,
With tearful eyes far gazing o'er the star-bespangled sea;
All alone, alone in sorrow, by the Rock of Branan-mor,
Behind her love's calm planet, and the sinking moon before.

II.

Nought beholds she as she gazes through the dim
  and windless west,
Save the diamond star-beams dancing o'er the sea's
  resplendent breast,
And the glorious changeful glitter of the shimmering splendour train,
From the shore, to where the bright moon hangs
  above the silent main.

III.

And she cries, " He is not coming! I have waited
  many a day
To see his white sail gleaming o'er the blue waves
  far away;
Many a midnight have I wept him with a sad heart
  mournfully,
But he cometh not, he cometh not, across the weary
  sea!"

IV.

The moon hangs o'er the water, with its face so calm
  and pale,
Now the lady looks beneath it, and she sees a rising
  sail,
And along that line of splendour comes a boat as
  bright as flame,
With a wondrous sheen all sparkling, as if out from
  Heaven it came!

V.

As a fragment from the morning is its light sail
  gleaming o'er,
Glow its smooth sides like the sunset, glitter diamonds in its prore;

By its mast a youth is sitting with an angel's beauty
  crowned,
And the lady shrieks with gladness, for her long-lost
  love is found!

FYTTE THE SECOND.

I.

Young Meergal of the Mountain, she sits all fond and
  fain,
With her own betrothed Garmon by the star-be-
  spangled main,
And she cries: "Oh! long lost rover, oh, beloved
  Garmon, tell
Why thou comest thus so strangely, in what bright
  land did'st thou dwell!

II.

For I've searched by strand and forest, I have waited
  many a day
By the deep, to see thy white sail o'er the blue waves
  far away;
Many a midnight have I wept thee, with a sad heart
  mournfully
Thinking, fearing thou wert lying 'neath the weary,
  weary sea!"

III.

" There was silence on the forest and the wide-spread
  burnished deep,
To the westward I was gazing from Brananmor the
  steep,
And I saw the Land of Glory through that sunset of
  the May,
Oh! the beautiful Hy Brasil", answered Garmon of
  the Bay.

IV.

"I pulled a blessed shamrock by the old saint's carven stone,
And I took my boat and faced her to Hy Brasil all alone,
And a gentle wind 'gan blowing as I left this iron shore,
And the sea grew ever brighter as I wafted swiftly o'er!

V.

Before me in the water, with a face like Heaven so fair,
Up rose the smiling Mermaid with her glossy golden hair,
And she gazed all gently on me, and she raised her queenly hand,
Pointing thro' the amber sunset to that far off heavenly land!

VI.

Still on, and on before me went that maiden of the wave,
My soul all drunk with pleasure at each piercing glance she gave,
And my heart all wildly throbbing at the witching smiles she wore,
'Till five boat-lengths scarce before me spread Hy Brasil's golden shore!

VII.

But 'twas all a land of shadows with the rainbow's radiance wove,
From the green sky-piercing mountain, to the sunny lowland grove;

Its lovely shore receded as my boat went swiftly on,
And the maiden of the ocean with the witching smiles was gone!

VIII.

I bethought me of the shamrock in its emerald glories drest,
With the earth still fresh upon it, and I took it from my breast;
I threw it to the breezes, and they bore it to the strand,
And it never more receded;—I trod the Enchanted Land!

IX.

A wild ecstatic wonder fills my soul since that strange day,
For I've walked with those enchanted in the ages past away;
And I've brought this boat of glory, oh! my lady love, for thee,
And we'll sail to calm Hy Brasil, and be blest eternally!"

FYTTE THE THIRD.

I.

'Tis Meergal of the Mountain that never more may weep,
For she sits beside her Garmon on the star-bespangled deep;
And in that boat of beauty are they sailing to the west,
With a love that lives eternal, toward the regions of the blest.

II.

And its many-tinted dwellers rose from out the deep's
  still domes,
To see what moving radiance glittered o'er their
  sparry homes;
And the dolphin heaved and gambolled around their
  glorious track,
With the sea one blaze of splendour where he showed
  his prismy back.

III.

Behind them rose the morning o'er a green and
  golden sea,
And that swift boat seemed its herald, it moved so
  gloriously;
And a sweet, unearthly music filled the atmosphere
  around,
On their ears for ever falling with a soul-entrancing
  sound.

IV.

It was the purple sunset when the breeze blew warm
  and bland,
And they saw a shore beyond them by its breath of
  fragrance fanned,
And within a heavenly harbour under hills serenely
  grand,
They have moored that boat of wonder in Hy Brasil's
  golden land.

V.

Up they wandered thro' the mountains from the
  broad cerulean sea,
'Till they reached a beauteous valley decked with
  many a fragrant tree.

As the countless stars that glitter on a cold December
 night,
Shone the flow'rs' gay-tinted blossoms o'er that
 valley of delight.

VI.

There a crystal stream danced downward with a
 wild melodious song,
And like children of the rainbow flew the warbling
 birds along;
Sang they sweetly as the wild harp when a master
 sweeps its wire,
As they flew from shore to greenwood, like gay
 sparks of heav'nly fire.

VII.

Like the deep blue depths of Heaven, when the
 April hours come on,
A lake, broad, calm, and glorious, 'mid that valley's
 bosom shone,
With its splendour-tinted islands, and their music-
 murmuring groves,
With its green encircling mountains, and its fairy
 strands and coves!

VIII.

On shore and shining island gleamed hall and
 palace gay,
Where dwell the blest Enchanted in cloudless joy
 alway;
Where roam the Fairy People thro' the scenes they
 like so well;
And, "Oh, love! oh, love!" said Garmon, "here for
 evermore we dwell!"

IX.

When the stars are on the waters, and the peasants
    by the shore,
Oft they see that boat of beauty with the sparkling
    diamond prore,
Sailing, sailing with the lovers o'er the silent mid-
    night sea,
To the beautiful Hy Brasil,* where they're blest
    eternally!

MARY LOMBARD.

I.

My iron gyves were rusty grown,
  So long I lay in thrall,
Down in my dungeon dark and lone,
  'Neath Kilnamulla's wall.

II.

My heavy chains at first were bright,
  But rust had dimmed them o'er,
When an angel came in the dead of night,
  And opened my dungeon door!

III.

Was never face so heavenly fair,
  As her's who let me go,
The lady of the sun-bright hair,
  The daughter of my foe.

---

* *Hy Brasil*—the Island of Atlantis—the Western Land, etc., is supposed to be identical with Tir-n-a-n Oge, the Paradise of the Pagan Irish. The peasantry believe they can still see it at sunset from the coasts of Clare, Galway, and Donegal. Brananmor is one of the highest pinnacles of the great precipice of Moher, on the coast of Clare.

IV.

She came as if from Heaven to me,—
　In the dead of night to my lair,—
And sped me to my own countrie,
　My Mary Lombard fair!

V.

When next where Kilnamulla rears
　Her towers now black and stern,
'Twas hosting with broad Thomond's spears,
　With Murrogh of the Fern.*

VI.

Through Desmond's plains with vengeful swords
　We carried war and flame,
And woe to all the Norman hordes,
　Where'er great Murrogh came.

VII

And all around that fated town
　Our warriors thronged full fain,
Till turret-stone and gate went down,
　Before their charge amain.

VIII.

Like a great flood, with flame and blood,
　We rushed through the breach's bound,
While roof and spire were wrapt in fire,
　Lighting the carnage round!

---

* In the year 1367 Murrogh na Ranagh, or Murrogh of the Fern, King of Thomond, issued from his fastnesses and destroyed nearly all the Norman strongholds in Munster; and after proclaiming himself King of the province, again crossed the Shannon. Buttevant, or as it was anciently called, Kilnamulla, was burnt and sacked by his forces in this war.

IX.

'Twas the gloom of night on the far-off height,
   'Twas the glare of hell round me,
As I stood before my foeman's door,
   His daughter fair to see.

X.

My foeman lay in the burning way,
   His fond wife dying there,
And my Mary dear, wild with woe and fear,
   I found on the great hall stair.

XI.

I clasped her in my arms, and then
   Quick bore her down the street,
Through the rushing men, to the eastward glen,
   Where I left my war-horse fleet.

XII.

A sudden madness seized my brain,
   And away I dashed, away,
With my trembling love towards my native plain
   By castle and mountain gray!

XIII.

Kilmallock's wall rose stark and tall
   On our course so wild and fast,
And the castle of Brugh frowned grimly through
   The darkness as we passed.

XIV.

At the morning's beam fair Shannon's stream
   A long length spread before:
I cared not its length, for love gave me strength,
   And I swam my war-horse o'er!

XV.

Away again, by valley and wild plain,
    Away through each torrent's foam,
Where the mountains rise, with my glorious maiden prize,
    Till I reached my castled home.

XVI.

One clasp I gave to my sad and sorrowing love,
    One word to my mother said,
And back, my loyalty to prove,
    To Murrogh's host I sped.

XVII.

Many a day, and many a weary night,
    And many a battle tough and stern,
I saw far, far from my true love bright,
    With Murrogh of the Fern.

XVIII.

And when he wore the crown of each plain and town,
    To my home at length I bore,
But my mother made her moan in its sad hall alone,
    For my Mary was sleeping evermore!

XIX.

Oh! my bright, tender flower, ever sat within her bower,
    Her mother and slain sire to mourn,
"Till sorrow quenched love's light, though it flamed up so bright,
    And she died, oh! she died, ere my return!

XX.

We laid her in her grave, where moans the mournful wave,—
    Oh! my long-loved and hard-earned bride!
There each day my watch I keep, and for ever long to sleep
    By my Mary Lombard's side!

THE SPALPEEN.

I.

When comes across the mountains the winter of the year,
With merry jokes and laughter the spalpeens gay are here;
I love the first of autumn, but more sweet Hallowe'en,
For it brings back my Johnnie, my rattling, gay Spalpeen.*

II.

His hair is like the raven that flies above Knockrue,
And stately is his form; his heart is kind and true,—
Oh! he's kindest, best, and bravest of all I've ever seen,
And until death I'll love him, my rattling, gay Spalpeen.

III.

There's something in my Johnnie that pains my secret mind;
He's statelier than his comrades, his manner's more refined;
I fear he's some rich rover, fit husband for a queen;
And yet I can't but love him, my rattling, gay Spalpeen!

IV.

The first night that I met him I found him fond and leal,
I took him for my partner and tripped a mazy reel,—

---

* The circumstance related in the ballad happened in the county Limerick. It was not at all an uncommon thing for wild young sons of the higher class of farmers to go off on their adventures, in the palmy days of potato-digging, with the spalpeens; and many a wild prank they played in their peregrinations.

It was the "New-mown Meadows", and then the
    light Moneen*
We danced—until I loved him, my rattling, gay Spal-
    peen!

V.

The leaves of dying autumn by chilling winds were
    tost,
The corn was stacked securely, the hills were gray
    with frost,
When by the turf-fire blazing, were met at Hallow-
    e'en
The farmers' sons and daughters, and many a gay
    Spalpeen.

VI.

The old man in the corner sat in his elbow chair;
At all his jokes the laughter rose free from grief or
    care;
The *Bean-a-thee*† sat smiling, and said she ne'er had
    seen
A dancer like young Johnnie, the rattling, gay Spal-
    peen.

VII.

They've laughed round many an apple, they've burned
    the nuts in glee,
"And some will soon get married, and some will sail
    the sea!"
They've danced for th' ancient piper, they've joked
    and sung between,
And told their wondrous legends, each rattling, gay
    Spalpeen!

---

* *Moneen*, a kind of jig—the wildest, most athletic, and spirited of all the Irish dances.

† *Bean-a-thee*, the woman of the house.

VIII.

Then Johnnie took the daughter, the eldest, by the hand,—
It was his own Bawn Ellen, the fairest in the land;
He led her towards her parents with fond and manly mien,
While all stood hushed around him, the rattling, gay Spalpeen!

IX.

"I've come across the mountains far, far from home to find
A wife above all others, both simple, fair, and kind;
She's standing now beside me, the loveliest I have seen!"
Up spoke with manly bearing, the rattling, gay Spalpeen.

X.

"I know she's good and constant—for me would lose her life:
I have a home to give her, and ask her for my wife!"
He's doffed the old gray garment—before them all is seen
The lord of many a townland, that rattling, gay Spalpeen!

XI.

Old Father James came early, and blessed the loving pair;
She's off with her dear bridegroom towards Kerry's hills so fair;
O'er many a fertile valley she reigns just like a queen,
Loving, and loved by, Johnnie, her rattling, gay Spalpeen!

MAUD OF DESMOND.

I.

Maud of Desmond ne'er again,
   Ne'er again shall wake to love:
She hath fled from grief and pain
   Away to Heaven's bright fields above—
Never more shall wake to love,
   Dreams a knight by a torrent narrow;
'Tis far down in the summer grove,
   By the dancing tide of the murmuring Carrow.

II.

Who is he, so fraught with pain,
   That dreams 'neath summer branches there?
The dark-haired knight of Castlemain,
   Of the stalworth frame and the stately air.
His brow is clouded now with care,
   They pierce his heart, these dreams, and harrow,
And he starteth up from his mossy lair
   By the dancing tide of the murmuring Carrow.

III.

Maud of Desmond loved him true,
   But, ah, her princely father smiled
On a stranger lord, who came to woo
   That bonnie maid so pure and mild.
Grim was the smile the young knight smiled;
   This touched his heart like a poisoned arrow,
As he dashed away on his charger wild
   From the dancing tide of the murmuring Carrow!

IV.

Maud of Desmond makes her moan
  For her hapless love in her native bowers:
The grand eve from its golden throne
  Is marshalling its crimson powers:
The fields beneath are starred with flowers,
  The stream runs calm where the aspens quiver;
It is where Crom's embattled towers
  Are mirrored in the Maig's bright river.

V.

She sees a knight come from the west
  Down the woody valley in fiery speed,
And well she knows his helmet crest,
  And the stately step of his gallant steed.
It is her own true knight, I rede,
  That comes his loving vows to give her,
And he sits beside her in the mead,
  That summer mead by the Maig's bright river.

VI.

And soon the young knight's vows are told,
  And soon he turns to the hills away,
But who, advancing from the wold,
  Bars his path to their summits gray?
It is the stranger lord,—all day
  He'd chased the roe where the wild woods quiver
To the bugle's note and the staghound's bay,
  In the summer dells by the Maig's bright river.

VII.

He stands within the woodland path,
  Glowering grim on the western knight,
And meeting in their hate and wrath,
  They close in stern and deadly fight;

There, in the reddening sunset light,
   Their keen swords into fragments shiver,
And they draw their daggers sharp and bright
   For that lady's love, by the Maig's deep river.

VIII.

Full short and deadly is the strife:
   The stranger lord is down, and there,
With outstretched hands he begs for life,—
   The young knight listens to his prayer,
And speaks with a calm and lordly air;—
   "Ho! take thy life, but shun the giver,
Shun the paths of this lady fair,
   For evermore by the Maig's bright river!"

IX.

"By the towers of Crom!" Earl Desmond cries,
   For he saw the strife from his castle wall—
"Such valour still my heart must prize
   'Till death upon its throbbings fall;
Ho! spread the banquet in the hall,
   The brave must have their meed for ever "
And he brings the knight to his festival
   In castled Crom, by the Maig's bright river!

X.

There was a mighty feast that e'en,
   A bridal train next morning tide,
And gladsome was the young knight's mien
   With Maud of Desmond at his side;
And oh! she was a happy bride,
   With all that power and love could give her,—
The fairest bride mid that region wide,
   In castled Crom by the Maig's bright river!

THE BURNING OF KILCOLEMAN.

I.

No sound of life was coming
 From glen, or tree, or brake,
Save the bittern's hollow booming
 Up from the reedy lake;
The golden light of sunset
 Was swallowed in the deep,
And the night came down with a sullen frown,
 On Houra's craggy steep.

II.

And Houra's hills are soundless:
 But hark, that trumpet blast!
It fills the forest boundless,
 Rings round the summits vast;
'Tis answered by another
 From the crest of Corrin Mór,
And hark again the pipe's wild strain
 By Bregoge's caverned shore!

III.

Oh! sweet at hush of even
 The trumpet's golden thrill,
Grand 'neath the starry Heaven
 The pibroch wild and shrill!
Yet all were pale with terror,
 The fearful and the bold,
Who heard its tone that twilight lone
 In the Poet's frowning hold!"*

---

* Kilcoleman Castle—an ancient and very picturesque ruin, once the residence of Spenser, lies on the shore of a small lake, about two miles to the west of Doneraile, in the county Cork. It belonged once to the Earls of Desmond, and was burned by their followers in 1598. Spenser, who was hated

IV.

Well might their hearts be beating;
    For up the mountain pass,
By lake and river meeting,
    Came kern and galloglass,
Breathing vengeance deadly
    Under the forest tree,
To the wizard man who cast the ban
    On the minstrels bold and free!

V.

They gave no word of warning,
    Round still they came, and on,
Door, wall, and rampart scorning—
    They knew not he was gone!
Gone fast and far that even,
    All secret as the wind,
His treasures all in that castle tall,
    And his infant son behind!

VI.

All still that castle hoarest—
    Their pipes and horn were still,
While gazed they through the forest,
    Up glen and northern hill;
'Till from the Brehon circle,*
    On Corrin's crest of stone,
A sheet of fire like an Indian pyre
    Up to the clouds was thrown.

---

by the Irish in consequence of his stringent advices to the English about the management of the refractory chiefs and minstrels, narrowly escaped with his life, and an infant child of his, unfortunately left behind, was burnt to death in the flames.

* On the summit of Corrin Mór, one of the Ballyhoura mountains, is a large circle of stones, in the centre of which rises a loose conical pile of small rocks. It was most probably a Brehon circle or judgment seat.

VII.

Then, with a mighty blazing,
    They answered—to the sky—
It dazzled their own gazing,
    So bright it rolled and high;
The castle of the Poet,—
    The man of endless fame,—
Soon hid its head in a mantle red
    Of fierce and rushing flame.

VIII.

Out burst the vassals, praying
    For mercy as they sped—
" Where was their master staying—
    Where was the Poet fled ?"
But hark! that thrilling screaming,
    Over the crackling din,—
'Tis the Poet's child in its terror wild,
    The blazing tower within!

IX.

There was a warlike giant
    Amid the listening throng,
He looked with face defiant
    On the flames so wild and strong,
Then rushed into the castle,
    And up the rocky stair,
But alas, alas, he could not pass
    To the burning infant there!

X.

The wall was tottering under,
    And the flame was whirring round,
The wall went down in thunder
    And dashed him to the ground;

Up in the burning chamber,
  For ever died that scream,
And the fire sprang out with a wilder shout,
  And a fiercer, ghastlier gleam!

XI.

It glared o'er hill and hollow,
  Up many a rocky bar,
From ancient Kilnamulla
  To Darra's Peak afar;
Then it heaved into the darkness
  With a final roar amain,
And sank in gloom with a whirring boom,
  And all was dark again!

XII.

Away sped the galloglasses
  And kerns, all still again,
Through Houra's lonely passes,
  Wild, fierce, and reckless men.
But such the Saxon made them,
  Poor sons of war and woe;
So they venged their strife with flame and knife
  On his head long, long ago!

ROMANCE OF THE GOLDEN SPURS.

I.

"I am weary, I am weary of the lagging hours alway,
The wound I got last autumn it pains me sore to-day—
'Tis burning and 'tis paining worse than when 'twas wet with gore,
And the joy of peace or battle I never shall see more".

II.

Thus spoke the brave Sir Thomas, the knight of Imokeel:
Beneath the Desmond's banner he'd drawn his conquering steel;
But out beneath that banner he never more may ride,
With that shot-maimed arm of valour, and that lance-head in his side.

III.

"My gallant boy, come hither—I give thee my brave steed,
My trusty blade I give thee to serve thee in thy need;
Then don thy battle harness, and with thy following ride
To join the noble Desmond by Imokeely's side!"

IV.

Then out and spake the mother—a fond and fair ladye—
"If I should lose my Gerald, oh! what can comfort me?
If I should lose my Gerald—if slain my boy should be,
One hour of peace or happiness I never more can see!"

V.

But nathless her beseeching, and nathless sigh and tear,
Young Gerald's gone to battle with many a gallant spear;

And in the early morning, by Bride's resounding wave,
They mark the sunbeams glancing from hostile helm and glaive.

VI.

"Come hither, oh! come hither, thou stripling young and gay",—
'Twas thus upon the hill-side the Desmond bold did say,—
"We'll down upon yon army: God wot, we'll give them play:
Go thou and take their castle, and win thy spurs to-day!"

VII.

It was above the bridge-end that castle proud did stand;
It was a gallant fortress as e'er was in the land;
And downward dashed young Gerald at his brave lord's command,
With his fearless ranks behind him, and his long glaive in his hand!

VIII.

He's leapt the fosse so bravely, 'mid shot and smoke and wrack;
He's mounted to the ramparts, his brave men at his back;—
They've ta'en the gallant fortress at the good point of the steel;
But where is he, their leader, the Boy of Imokeel?

IX.

They've searched round fosse and rampart, but cannot find him there;
They've searched the batter'd chambers, and up the gory stair,

'Till by the turret window, with his helmet cleft in twain,
They've found their young commander, 'mid a circle of the slain!

X.

It was a day of triumph to the Desmond by that shore,
And yet a day of sorrow when young Gerald up they bore—
Up they bore unto the hill-side, where the noble Desmond stood,
With his golden banner o'er him, stained with many a foeman's blood.

XI.

Then out and spoke the Desmond: "Ho! list ye all to me!
This boy has ta'en the castle—this boy a knight shall be;
But the hue of death's upon him, and he cannot speak or kneel—
Ho! page, my spurs, unbrace them, and fix them on his heel!"

XII.

I wis the sight was woeful, e'en in that foughten place,
With the red gash on his forehead, and the blood on his pale face,
With the golden spurs braced on him, glittering in the sunlight clear,
Beneath that rustling banner, stretch'd upon his gory bier!

XIII.

Thro' Imokeel they bore him, 'cross many a plain and dell,
They bore him to his father, and told him how he fell;
The old man's wound burst open, and the blood welled from his side,
And he kissed his pale young champion, and down he sank and died!

XIV.

"Now leave me", said the mother, as wild she made her moan,—
"Now leave me in this chamber to my great grief alone!"
And she raised her voice in wailing till the twilight gathered down
Upon her leafy forests, and her hills and moorlands brown.

XV.

It was the starry midnight ere the mother's tones sank low,
And she prayed unto our Lady with a broken voice and slow:—
"Oh! thou who once wert stricken worse than I, long, long ago,
Prop me up in this great trial, give me strength to bear my woe".

XVI.

What breaks the heavy stillness? what in the chamber stirs?
Sure she hears the clank of armour, and the clink of those bright spurs!

And she looks upon her Gerald with a thrill of joy
    and fear,
For he's rising, rising slowly, in his armour from
    the bier.

XVII.

Oh! not slain, not slain, but wounded! Many a
    field of fire and steel
Saw those sharp spurs' golden brightness dimmed
    with gore upon each heel;
For in aftertime for Erin never one so true and leal
As Sir Gerald of the Forest, the Knight of Imokeel!

THE DYING WARRIOR.

I.

Brightly on the crest of Darra
Fell the day's last golden arrow,
    And the moon smiled radiantly,
    Calmly, lonely, mournfully,
On a leafy dell and narrow,
    Opening out towards green Fear-muighe.

II.

Low young Dermuid there is lying,
Listening to the foemen flying,
    For the close and bloody fray,
    In the Red Gap raged all day—
Ah! that hapless youth is dying
    In the pale moon's mournful ray!

III.

There his rushing comrades left him,
When the struggling foemen cleft him—

Cleft him through helmet bright,
As he swept upon their flight—
Ah! that fatal blow has reft him
Of the joy he hoped that night.

IV.

For beside his native forest,
In the abbey old and hoarest,
   Wife he was that night to call
   The fairest maid in cot or hall;
And that thought afflicts him sorest,
   On the brink of bliss to fall!

V.

" Death", he cries, " doth point his arrow—
Make my bed so cold and narrow,
   Where the sunlight falls in gold
   On Glenroe's bright stream and wold,
'Neath the haunted Peak of Darra,
   In the abbey gray and old!

VI.

Thou, thy bridal dress adorning,
When the war-scout gave the warning,—
   When thou find'st thy Dermuid slain,
   Kiss his cold brow once again,—
Thou wilt have at dawn of morning
   Face of woe and heart of pain!"

VII.

In that dell, like fairies glancing,
Wildly the young fawns are dancing,
   And the limping hares out-tread,
   All their daylight terrors fled;
But none scares their bold advancing,
   For the warrior youth is dead!

VIII.

In that dell at morn's first peeping,
Mad with sorrow, worn with weeping,
  Mary bends the dead above;
  He died in war,—she soon for love;
And side by side the twain are sleeping,
  'Neath the abbey's haunted grove!

SIR DOMNALL.

I.

Afar in the vales of green Houra my heart lingers all the day long,
Mid the dance of the light-footed maidens, with the music of Ounanar's song,
Where the steep hills uprise all empurpled with the bloom of the bright heather bells,
Looking down on their murmuring daughters, the blue streams of Houra's wild dells!
In the hush of a calm summer sunset, where sing these sweet streams as they flow,
As I sat with the bright-eyed young maidens, they made me their bard long ago;
Then I told of each valley some story, some tale of each blue mountain crest,
But they loved of all wild tales I sang them the lay of Sir Domnall the best;
So I'll sing once again of his deeds in my boyhood's rude measures and rhymes,—
Then, gentles, all list to the story, this lay of the old chivalric times!

II.

Nigh the shores of the loud-sounding **Bregoge**, high
    towering o'er valley and wold,
Walled in by the rough steeps of Houra, there
    standeth a gray feudal hold;
It is worn by the hard hail of battle, decay is at
    work on its hill,
Yet it stands like a sorrow-struck Titan, high, lone,
    and unconquer'ble still!
The green ivy clingeth around it, the blast is at play
    in its halls,
The weasel peeps forth from its crannies, the black
    raven croaks on its walls;
The peasants who pass in the even will hurry their
    steps from its height,
For they tell fearful things of its chambers, and call
    it the Tower of the Sprite!*
But though lone be its halls, they rang merry with
    wassail and minstrel's wild lay,
When it sheltered the youthful Sir Domnall, its lord
    in the good olden day!

III.

Oh! he was a brave forest knight! As each morn-
    ing upsprang from the sea,
He was out by the fay-haunted streams, with his
    falcons, in woody Fear-muighe;

---

* Along the northern confines of Fear-Muighe-Feine run the Houra mountains, in the midst of which the Ounanar river rises, and flowing through a magnificent glen—Gleann-an-awr, or the Valley of Slaughter—falls into the Oubeg or Mulla, below Doneraile. The Bregoge, another tributary of the Oubeg, has its source also in these mountains; and near its banks, a few miles north-east of Doneraile, stands the ancient Castle Phooka—the "'Tower of the Sprite'.

Or away, far away mid the mountains, with stag-
    hound, and bugle, and steed,
O'er-matching the gray wolf in boldness, outstrip-
    ping the red deer in speed!
And his heart and his strong hand were bravest;
    when high rose the trumpet's wild strain,
When the war-fires blazed red on the hill-tops, and
    the horsemen rode hard on the plain,
He was dight in his harness and spurring to the
    Desmond's bright banner away,
His mountaineers dashing behind him, with sabres
    athirst for the fray!
In bower and in hall he was welcomed, and the
    dames of the crag castles brave
Were proud when he smiled on their daughters, at
    eve by the Avonmore's wave!

IV.

'Tis noon on the broad plain of Limerick, and down
    by the calm Lubach's tide,*
The sunbeams smite hot on the meadows, and burn
    by the green forest side;
And brightly they glint from a helmet, and broadly
    they gleam from a shield,
Where a knight rideth up by the river in brave
    shining panoply steeled.
Kerne crouch on his path in the greenwood, with
    pikes ready raised for a foe,
But they know the high mien of Sir Domnall, and
    stay for some Saxon the blow;
And the galloglach scowls from his ambush; but he
    too remembers that plume,
And wishing good luck to its owner, strides back to
    his lair in the gloom.

---

* *Lubach*—the Winding River—the stream that runs by Kilmallock.

But why rides Sir Domnall so lonely, and why is his
    gladness all fled?
On a field by Lough Gur's lonely water the friend
    of his bosom lies dead!

V.

Away, then, away to the mountains, he giveth his
    war-horse the rein,
While he longs for the clangour of battle, to drown
    his dejection again;
The blest Hill of Patrick* slopes green with its tall
    Guebre tower on his way,
But the good monk who waits in the abbey in vain
    looketh out for his stay;
And anon the black Rock of the Eagle frowns down
    on his path by Easmore,
'Till he crosseth the bright Oun-na-Geeraith, and
    windeth away by its shore.
Now nigh him Suidhe Fein riseth proudly o'er wild
    Glenisheen's ancient wood;
And yawns like a gate in the mountains, Red Shard's
    Gap of conflict and blood;
As he turns by the crags of Sliav Fadha, and on by
    a flat moorland side,
Till he lights nigh a clear fairy fountain at length by
    the Ounanar's tide.

VI.

It is on a small shrubby islet with huge forest cliffs
    all around,
Save where the bright stream from the blue hills
    outleaps with a lone, lulling sound;

---

* *Ard Patrick*—the Height of St. Patrick—is a beautiful green hill at the Limerick side of the Houras. On its summit is an ancient church, the time of whose foundation is unknown. Near the church are the remains of a round tower which fell nearly half a century ago.

And it seems as if step of nought human did e'er on
    its low strand alight ;
Yet a lady peers out from the thicket beyond the
    good steed of the knight !
She is old, yet there's fire in her dark eye, but sor-
    row is stamped on her mien,
And she knows the tall crest of Sir Domnall, and
    comes to his side from the screen ;
She waveth her hand to him sadly ; he follows her
    steps by the flood,
Till they enter a hut of thick brambles concealed in
    the dark spreading wood,
And there, on a couch of green fern, an old dying
    chieftain is laid,
And o'er him in wild, bitter weeping there bendeth
    a golden-haired maid.

VII.

He turns to the knight as he enters, and thus in
    weak accents of woe :—
"Thy sire was my friend, good Sir Domnall, in the
    days of our youth long ago ;
The Saxon hath slaughtered my people,—alas for
    that gloom-darkened hour,
When he forced me to fly, weak and wounded, thus
    far from Du Aragail's tower !*
A friend, ah ! a friend false and hollow, hath tracked
    me to Ounanar's grove,
And he swears on his sword to betray me, or have
    this young maid for his love ;

---

* Du Aragail, an ancient castle in the parish of Dromagh, near Kanturk, was one of the principal seats of the O'Keeffes. *Kilnamulloch*—the "Church of the Curse"—the ancient name of Buttevant. An extremely wild legend is connected with this name. Rathgogan is the ancient name of Charleville.

Black Murrogh, stern lord of Rathgogan! soon, soon from thy wiles I am free,
But alas for the wife of my bosom,—alas, my fair daughter, for thee!"
He died on that eve, and was borne away to the age-honoured spires
Of gray Kilnamulloch next noontide, and laid down to rest with his sires.

VIII.

There was feasting that night in Kilcoleman, and all in their bright martial gear,
Black Murrogh, and fearless Sir Domnall, and many stout champions are there;
And there speaks Sir Domnall, uprising, and bends on black Murrogh his gaze:—
"Ho! freres of the feast and the battle, a tale of the wild forest maze!
As I rode by the Ounanar's water, Du Aragail's chieftain I found,
He was driven from his home by the Saxon, and said, ere he died of his wound:
'A friend, ah! a friend false and hollow, has tracked me to Ounanar's side,—
A friend who has sworn to betray me, or have my young daughter his bride!'
By my faith! but the traitor was knightly, to woo her with ardour so brave;
Now, there lies my gauntlet before him; thus proof of his passion I crave!"

IX.

Then up starts the lord of Rathgogan, and fierce is the flash of his eye,
As he glares on the dark brows around him with bearing defiant and high:

"False knight of a falser young maiden, thy gauntlet I take from the board,
And soon on thy crest in the combat I'll prove my good name with my sword;
For I see but one path to my glory, a path o'er that false heart of thine,
But fired by the love of young damsels, but steeled by the red gushing wine;
And close be the palisade round us, and short be the distance between,
Where a liar's black life-blood shall poison the bloom of the bright summer green!"
"And fair shine the sun", quoth Sir Domnall, "the clear sunny sheen on my blade,
When I close with the lord of Rathgogan, avenging Du Aragail's maid!"

X.

Calm eve on the fair hills of Houra, and down by the Mulla's green marge,
The red beams are burning in glory from hauberk, and sabre, and targe,
And the warriors are circling around it, that smooth listed green by the wave,
Where the two mailëd champions are standing with keen axe, and target, and glaive!
Flash lances around them in brightness, gleam banners along by the shore,
Fierce Condon's from Araglin's water, De Rupe's from the towers of Glenore;
And the Barry's wild pennon is waving, and the flags of the chieftains whose towers
Defy from their crag-seats the foeman by Avonmore's gorges and bowers;
Yet still the two champions stand moveless, all silent and darkly the while,
Like the panoplied statues that frown round the walls of some gray abbey aisle!

XI.

But hark! how the wild martial trumpets outroll
    the fierce signal for strife!
And see how these motionless statues outstart from
    their postures to life!
The mailed heels go round on the green-sward, the
    mailed hands ply weapons amain,
Till the targes are battered and cloven, and the axes
    are shivered in twain!
Wide and deep are the wounds of Sir Domnall, but
    wider the gash of his foe,
As their sabres cross gleaming and clashing—two
    flames in the red sunny glow—
One thrust through the blood-spattered hauberk, one
    stroke by the crest waving o'er,
And the lord of Rathgogan lies fallen, to rise to the
    combat no more;
And there for a space swaying, reeling, and faint
    from his wounds' gushing tide,
Sir Domnall looks down on the vanquished, then
    sinketh to earth by his side!

XII.

They bear one away to his tower, and they bear one
    away stark and cold;
One ne'er may awake, and one waketh, a bright,
    blessed scene to behold;
For the maid of Du Aragail bendeth above the dim
    couch where he lies,
With love as her spirit immortal, and joy like the
    morn in her eyes!
Oh! sweet are the dreams of his slumbers, o'erflow-
    ing with fairy delight,
But sweeter the dreams of his waking each day in
    the Tower of the Sprite.

And now 'tis the fulness of summer—a fair breezy
    morning in June,
And the streams of green Houra are leaping along
    with a sweet gushing tune,
And thy bells, Kilnamulloch, are ringing—no knells
    of the bloom-footed hours—
But the sweet bridal chimes of Sir Domnal and the
    maid of Du Aragail's towers!

THE BARON AND THE MILLER.

I.

There was a steed, a brave black steed,
    Lithe of body and limb,
And in country or town, for strength or speed,
    There never was one like him.

II.

He had sinews of brass for the chase's flight,
    Eyes of fire as he swept the hill,
He'd a heart of steel for the bloody fight;
    And his master was Aodh of the Mill.

III.

But Aodh of the Mill had a master too,
    The Baron of Darenlawr,*
Whom he served in peace as a vassal should do,
    And followed in day of war.

---

* Of this ancient castle but one tower, now completely covered with ivy, remains. It stands on the southern bank of the Suir, in the county Waterford, about two Irish miles eastward of Clonmel. The foundations, on arches, can yet be discerned, and from their extent and thickness, it must have been once a fortress of great strength and importance. It was garrisoned for the English, in the days of Queen Elizabeth, by the Butlers, to whom it belonged. The scenery around it is very beautiful and romantic.

IV.

Never were twain, by hill or by plain,
   So matched in passion and ill,
As the baron bold of that castle old
   And his vassal, wild Aodh of the Mill.

V.

By Cummeragh one morn, with stag-hound and horn,
   They hunted like the wind,
But the black, black steed, with his sinews of speed,
   Left the ireful baron's behind.

VI.

"This brown steed of mine, wild Aodh, shall be thine,
   With fifty crowns so bright;
But I must have thy charger brave,
   For I need his strength in the fight!"

VII.

Then out and told that miller so bold:
   "I care not for favour or pelf;
And this brave steed of mine shall never be thine,
   For I need his strength myself!"

VIII.

Then an ireful man was the dark baron,
   And an angry laugh he gave:
"I will have thy steed, tho' the demon should feed
   On thy carcass, thou grinding knave!"

IX.

And tho' Aodh was strong, down, down to the Earth,
   The vassals they've dragged him amain,
And they've changed each saddle, and rein, and girth,
   And mounted him once again.

X.

On the baron's brown horse now he's mounted per force,
   And the baron sits on the other;
The baron is glad, but the miller is mad
   With a passion he cannot smother!

XI.

He digs the spurs in the brown steed's sides
   Till it snorts with rage and pain,
Then up with a fiendish frown he rides
   To the baron's bridle rein.

XII.

"May the memory of crime thy bosom freeze,—
   The worm that never dies—
Till the flames of Hell on thy dark soul seize,
   And I see it with mine eyes!"

XII.

Then he plunges and volts, and away he bolts,
   And down the rough mountain he's gone;
While the vassals' laughter rings wildly after,
   And the shout of the fierce baron.

XIV.

There were battles enough both bloody and tough,
   To employ them both, I wot,
And swift moons ran over master and man,
   Till the curse was all forgot.

XV.

But there came a day when the baron lay
   On his bed of sickness and dole,
And the bells were rung at the evening gray
   For his departing soul.

XVI.

There came three knocks to the miller's gate
   In the dead hour of the night,
And the miller he rose at a furious rate,
   And looked in the dim moon's light.

XVII.

And there sat the Baron of Darenlawr
   Upon the swift black horse,
And his fixed eyes glared 'neath his visor bar,
   And his brow was pale as a corse!

XVIII.

"Come hither! come hither! thou miller brave,—
   Ho! mount and follow me!"
On the dark brown steed Aodh is mounted with speed,
And away with the Baron is he.

XIX.

In their garb of war by old Darenlawr,
   And down by the rushing Suir,
'Till they strike on a track, all barren and black,
   O'er a wide and lonely moor.

XX.

Black mountains rise to the pale dim skies,
   Beyond that desert place,
As side by side away they ride
   In a fierce and furious race.

XXI.

Taller and taller each giant hill,
   And darker their chasms grow,
As away over quagmire and brawling rill
   Like demons of night they go.

XXII.

Redder and redder the Baron's eyes glared,
  But 'twas more from rage than fear,
As the bog-fiend's lamp on their pathway flared,
  And they swept that barrier near.

XXIII.

And there at last rose a crag so vast
  That it hid in the clouds its face;
Then the miller reined in, but the baron spurred past
  Till he neared its gloomy base.

XXIV.

Then it rocked and shaked and it groaned and quaked,
  And its breast burst right before,
And a mighty flame thro' the broad rent came
  As from Hell's eternal door!

XXV.

Yet on and on spurred the fierce baron,
  Till he came to that fiery rent
Then his teeth he ground, and with one great bound
  Thro' its flaming throat he went!

XXVI.

One hellish roar thro' the heavens tore
  As the rent up closed again,
And the bog-fiend's lamp went out on the swamp,
  And the black cocks crowed by the fen!

XXVII.

The miller he rose at the break of day,
    And looked for the rock and the moor—
Nought before him lay but that castle gray
    And his own blithe mill by the Suir.

XXVIII.

Then he crossed the mill weir furiously,
    And quick to the stable he sped;
But an humbled and awe-struck man was he
    When he found his steed stark dead!

XXIX.

Then sore of body and weary of bone,
    To Derenlawr he passed,—
From its gloomy halls rose the vassals' moan,
    For the baron was gone at last.

XXX.

" And now, oh! now, my brave black steed,
    I'll have thee!" the miller said,
As he sought the stable with eager speed;
    But the black steed too was dead!

THE TAKING OF ARMAGH.

A.D. 1596.

I.

'Twas fast by grey Killoter we made the Saxons run,
We hewed them with the claymore, and smote them with the gun.
"Armagh! Armagh!" cried Norris, as wild he spurred away,
And sore beset and scattered, they reached its walls that day!

II.

Alas! we had no cannon to batter down the gate,
To level fosse and rampart, so we were forced to wait,
And 'leaguer late and early that place of old renown,
By dint of plague and famine to bring the foeman down.

III.

Then up and spake our general, the great and fearless Hugh:
"We'll give them fit amusement while we've nought else to do;
Then deftly ply your bullets, and pick the warders down,
And well watch pass and togher that none may leave the town".

IV.

We camped amid the valleys and bonnie woods about,
But spite of all our watching, one gallant wight got out,

Till far Dundalk he entered by spurring day and
    night,
And told them of our leaguer, and all their woeful
    plight.

V.

Then Norris raised his gauntlet, and smote his
    mailéd breast—
"God curse these northern rebels with fire and
    plague and pest!
Ho! captain of the arsenal, send food and succour
    forth,
For if we lose that stronghold, the Queen must lose
    the North!"

VI.

'Twas on a stormy twilight, when wildly roared the
    blast,
Up to our prince's standard a scout came spurring
    fast,
And told him how that convoy—four hundred stal-
    worth men—
Had pitched their camp at sunset by Gartan's
    woody glen.

VII.

"Then let them take their slumber", said our great
    prince that night—
"God wot, they'll sleep far sounder before the
    morning's light:
My son, thou'rt ever yearning to win one meed—
    renown;
Go! if thou slay'st the convoy, then we will take the
    town!"

VIII.

He sprang upon his charger, our prince's gallant son,
And fast his path we followed, till Gartan's glen we won;
And there beside the torrent, with watch-fires burning low,
Deep in their fatal slumber, we spied the Saxon foe.

IX.

When booms the autumn thunder, and thickly pours the rain,
From Mourne's great mountain valley the flood sweeps o'er the plain—
While up our drums we rattled, and loud our trumpets blew,
Like that wild torrent swept we upon the Saxon crew!

X.

We swept upon their vanguard, we rushed on rere and flank,
Like corn before the sickle we mowed them rank on rank,
And ere the ghostly midnight we'd slain them every one—
I trow they slept far sounder before the morrow's dawn!

XI.

"Now don the convoy's garments, and take their standard too",—
'Twas thus at blink of morning out spake our gallant Hugh;

"And march ye toward the city, with baggage, arms,
    and all,
With all their promised succour, and see what shall
    befall!"

XII.

We donned their blood-red garments, and shook
    their banner free,
We marched us toward the city, a gallant sight to
    see;
Upon their drums we rattled the Saxon point of
    war,
And soon the foemen heard us, and answered from
    afar.

XIII.

From dreams of lordly banquets that morn the
    Saxons woke,
When on their ears our clamour of drums and
    trumpets broke;
And up they sprang full blithely, and crowded one
    and all,
Like lank wolves, gazing greedily from loop-hole,
    gate, and wall.

XIV.

There was an ancient abbey, a pile of ruined
    stone,
Two gun-shots from the ramparts, amid the wild
    woods lone;
And there he lay in ambush—our tanist brave and
    young—
And as we neared the city, upon our flank he
    sprung!

XV.

With all his rushing troopers out from the wood he
    sped,
Their matchlocks filled with powder—they did not
    want the lead—
And well they feigned the onset with shot and sabre
    stroke,
And deftly too we met them with clouds of harmless
    smoke!

XVI.

Some tossed them from their saddles to imitate the
    slain;
Whole ranks fell at each volley along the bloodless
    plain;
And groans and hollow murmurs of well-feigned
    woe and fear,
From that strange fight rang mournfully upon the
    foeman's ear!

XVII.

Up heaved the huge portcullis, round swang the
    ponderous gate,
Out rushed the foe to rescue, or share their com-
    rades' fate;
And fiercely waved their banners, and bright their
    lances shone,
And, "George for merry England!" they cried as
    they fell on.

XVIII.

Saint Columb! the storm of laughter that from our
    ranks arose,
As up the *corpses* started, and fell upon our foes;

As we, the routed convoy, closed up our thick ranks
 well,
And met the foe with claymore, red pike, and petronel!*

XIX.

'Twas then from out the forest our mighty chieftain
 came,
Like a fierce autumn tempest of roaring wind and
 flame—
So loud his horsemen thundered, and rang their
 slogan free,
And swept upon th' affrighted foe with all his
 chivalrie!

XX.

Yet stout retired the Saxon, though he was sore dis-
 trait,
'Till, with his ranks commingled, in burst we through
 the gate;
Then soon the Red Hand† fluttered upon their
 highest towers,
And wild we raised our triumph shout, for old
 Armagh was ours!

---

* Petronel, a long dag or pistol.
† The Red Hand, the device on the banner of Tyrone.

THE WELL OF THE OMEN.

I.

At morn up green Ard-Patrick the Sunday bell rang clear,
And downward came the peasants with looks of merry cheer,
With many a youth and maiden by pathways green and fair,
To hear the Mass devoutly and say the Sunday prayer;
And the meadows shone around them where the sky-larks gay were singing,
And the stream sang songs amid the flowers, and the Sunday bell was ringing.

II.

There is a well sunk deeply by old Ard-Patrick's wall,
Within it gaze the peasants to see what may befall:
Who see not there their shadows shall die within the year;
Who see their shadows smiling, oh! they'll have merry cheer!
There stayed the youths and maidens, where the soft green grass was springing,
While the stream sang songs amid the flowers, and the Sunday bell was ringing.

III.

Out spoke wild Rickard Hanlon, "We'll see what may befall"—
'Twas to young Bride Mac Donnell, the flower among them all,—

"Come see if ours be sorrow or merry wedlock's band!"
Then took the smiling maiden all by the lily hand,
And there they knelt together, their bright looks downward flinging,
While the stream sang songs amid the flowers, and the Sunday bell was ringing.

IV.

They looked into the water: no shadows shone below:
The dark, dark sign of evil! Ah! could it e'er be so?
Full lightly laughed young Rickard, although his heart was chill,
And with fair Bride Mac Donnell and all went down the hill,
To hear the Mass devoutly, with the soft airs round them winging,
While the stream sang songs amid the flowers, and the Sunday bell was ringing.

V.

Sweet months, despite the omen, in sunny bliss flew o'er,
And sometimes thinking on it but made them love the more;
But when across Ard-Patrick they sought the lowland plain,
Into the well's dark waters they never looked again,
There never with the maidens they sat, fair garlands stringing,
While the stream sang songs amid the flowers, and the Sunday bell was ringing.

*   *   *   *   *   *

VI.

The storm and flood were over—they left us wild dismay,
The Ford's great rocks were loosened 'neath Easmor's torrent gray,
And clasped in death together—oh, sad the tale to tell!
Were found young Bride and Rickard drowned by the Robber's Well!
O! false and cruel water, so merry downward flinging,
How canst thou sing amid the flowers while the death bell loud is ringing?

VII.

From old Ard-Patrick's ruins loud sounds the piercing keen;
By the sad Well of the Omen a deep, deep grave is seen,
Where side by side together they've laid the early dead,
And the Mass they've chaunted o'er them, and the requiem prayer is said;—
There was woe and bootless sorrow in many a bosom clinging,
But the stream sang songs amid the flowers while the death bell loud was ringing!

THE ENCHANTED WAR HORSE.

I.

Doon hangs above the ocean clear,
    A tower of towers the hoarest,
And rears its gray head, stern and drear,
    O'er inland vale and forest,

Deserted all for many a year,
   While the sun shone on the roses;
And the laugh of man shall never more
Resound within its chambers hoar,
While the wave rolls by with thundering force,
   Or at its base reposes,
While the linnet sings on the golden gorse,
   And the sun shines on the roses.

II.

The fairies dance on Doon's gray hill
   When the midnight moon shines brightly,
But they foot it too by its forest rill,
   With many a prank full sprightly;
They foot it round and dance their fill
   When the sun shines on the roses,
Within its weird-like forest maze,
Where the flowers with light are all ablaze,
Where the stream along its glittering course
   Full many a charm discloses,
And the linnet sings on the golden gorse,
   And the sun shines on the roses.

III.

With light clouds over Doon arrayed
   In summer skies serenest,
The fairies danced within a glade,
   The loneliest and the greenest,
Where rolled 'neath shimmering sun and shade
   A forest brook the sheenest,
And many a laugh rang to the sky,
And many a breeze went warbling by,
Gathering sweet perfumes in its course
   For all these fairy noses,
While the linnet sang on the golden gorse,
   And the sun shone on the roses.

IV.

And there danced Blanaid of the Wood,
   And there danced Maiv the Merry,
And Meergal Ban, the gay and good,
   With red lips like a cherry,
And Banba of the Snowy Hood,
   With cheeks like rowan berry,
And many another elf-maid bright,
And many a gallant fairy knight;
And loud and sweet the green trees o'er,
   Up rang their laughter ever,
Where frowned that castle grim and hoar,
   And sang the woodland river.

V.

A heavy tramp sounds thro' the copse,
   Upon their sport advancing,
And now their gleesome laughter stops,
   And now their merry dancing;
And treading down the lusmore tops
   A steed comes outward prancing—
A great gray steed with glossy back,
With crested mane of midnight black,
With archéd neck and mighty limb,
   And bold eyes glittering ever;
Where frowned that castle hoar and grim,
   And sang the woodland river.

VI.

They look into his great black eyes
   That gaze on them with wonder,
And now they talk in wild surprise,
   And now they pause and ponder;
At length a gallant elf-knight cries:
   " Out from the castle yonder,

We'll bring the armour that we found
Deep in the chamber under ground,
And with it send this steed of might
   A master seeking ever!"
Where frowned that castle on the height,
   And sang the woodland river.

VII.

With laugh and shout away they go,
   And up the steep rocks clamber;
They heed not that the sea below
   Lies stretched like golden amber;
They were too busy far, I trow;
   For, from the haunted chamber,
They've brought the armour forth, and braced
The saddle bright with silver chased,
The haunch-plates, breast-plate, forehead boss,
   And rein of golden glory,
Where the woodland stream sang thro' the moss,
   And frowned that castle hoary.

VIII.

They hung beside the saddle sheen
   A helm and lance, of lances
The best that e'er in war was seen
   Or heard of in romances;
And then they capered round the green,
   And then with merry glances
Upon the steed strange spells they laid,
And dancing round him in the glade,
Said, "Go thou forth, thou gallant horse,
   And find what fate discloses,
While the linnet sings on the golden gorse,
   And the sun shines on the roses!"

IX.

The steed sped down the forest straight,
   Came by a lordly castle,
Where all were noon and night elate
   With wine and roaring wassail;
A jolly knight came from the gate
   Bedecked with plume and tassel,
And sprang upon his back, but there
Soon went he flying through the air,
And down on earth with broken bones
   In grief and woe to languish,
And found that sermons lie in stones*
   Of bitter pain and anguish!

X.

Next by a castle prim and bare
   That great steed's hoofs came clanging,
Where rose the hypocritic prayer
   And hymns with nasal twanging;
Its lord came down the castle stair,
   His godly bosom banging,
And sprang upon the horse's back,
But soon went prone into the black
Deep moat, where oft his holy steel
   Strewed poor malignants' corses,
And found his hypocritic zeal
   Was most unfit for horses!

XI.

By tower and street the country round,
   By many a hall of pleasure,
He sped, but every rider found
   Wanting in some sad measure;
One was a miser whom he drowned
   With all his bags of treasure,

---

* " Sermons in stones, and good in everything"—*Shakspeare.*

One was a knave that sold his cause,
And one a bloody tyrant was;
Another was a false mean hack,
    Of great men's views the ranter:
But all, as each one gained his back,
    He hurled to earth instanter!

XII.

At length by lone Cragbarna's side,
    A region Ossianic,
Where none but outlaws dared abide,
    Mid horrid rocks volcanic;
As gaily on the great steed hied,
    Down from a crag Titanic
A young knight sprang—'twas John the Brown,
The banished lord of Barnaloun—
Upon his back, and stuck thereon
    As firm as any Persian
That ever rode beneath the sun
    In battle or diversion!

XIII.

The great steed plunged and reared amain
    To cause some dire disaster,
And 'cross the crags did wildly strain,
    And down the steep gorge faster;
But every ruse he tried in vain,
    For faith he'd found his master—
He'd found a knight full brave and true,
Whose heart no foul dishonour knew,
Whose sword was drawn to sweep each curse
    Away that wrong imposes,
While the linnet sang on the golden gorse,
    And the sun shone on the roses!

XIV.

And gaily cried Sir John the Brown,
   As like a lamb, or tamer,
The steed at last trode mildly down:
   "Oh! now I'm free to name her,—
My ladye love of bright renown,—
   To worship and to claim her
To be my bride, for with this fine
Brave steed I'll win what should be mine,
My native hall, my broad domain
   That every charm discloses,
While the linnet sings his merry strain,
   And the sun shines on the roses!"

XV.

Then rode he round full furiously,
   And called up friend and vassal,
And drew them on the enemy
   That held his native castle;
And there all were eternally
   Immersed in wine and wassail,
And knew not, heard not, till they saw
Sir John the Brown his good sword draw
Before the gate, on that great horse,
   To slit their traitorous noses,
While the linnet sang on the golden gorse,
   And the sun shone on the roses!

XVI.

Sir John the Brown his home hath won,
   And thrashed the foemen fairly:
His ladye love of bright renown
   He made his bride full early;
Brave lord and lady both are gone;
   Their castle looms all drearly,

A ruin stark and lone, but still
The peasant hears upon its hill
The tramp of that great wizard horse,
   And will while men have noses,
While the linnet sings on the golden gorse,
   And the sun shines on the roses!

THE PILGRIM.

I.

As I sat at the cross in the village, it was on a bright summer day,
An old man came silently thither, was drooping, and bearded, and gray;
There was dust on his shoon and his garments, the sore dust of many a mile:—
"Oh! where are you going, gray pilgrim? Come rest 'neath this green tree a-while!"

II.

"Oh! God's holy blessing be on you! an hour from my journey I'll steal:
I have wandered from morning till noon-tide, and foot-sore and weary I feel;
I am going fast, fast to the grave-yard, and wish I may reach it full soon,
'Till under its green grass untroubled I sleep by my Aileen Aroon!

III.

"Oh! she was an Orangeman's daughter, but wild was her fondness for me;
She dwelt where in glory and splendour broad Barrow sweeps down to the sea;

She was fair as the roses of summer, and mild as a
  May morning bland;
Oh! a maiden so bright in her beauty was never
  like her in the land.

IV.

"Ah! darkly and sore I remember it was in the
  wild ninety-eight,
When peace from our land was uprooted, and sad
  was the poor peasant's fate;
I'd scarce numbered twenty fair summers, the blood
  ran like fire in my veins,
And I rose with the rest for old Ireland, to free her
  from bondage and chains.

V.

"I had a strange power 'mong my neighbours: my
  sires had been lords in the land:
And soon on the hills round me gathered a reckless,
  a wild daring band:
Thro' many a sad scene I led them, by lone cot and
  strife-ruined hall,
Till a dark hour of gloom saw me faithless to God
  and my country and all!

VI.

"In the madness of love I had promised, the last
  time I parted my dear,
That I'd ne'er draw the sword 'gainst her father,
  when met in the battle's career;
I kept to that promise too truly, betrayed with old
  Ireland my trust,
And my name was soon named with the traitors, and
  my idol soon crumbled to dust!

VII.

"We'd camped in a gorge of the mountains: the
  red-coats and yeomen were nigh;
'If I wait for the morning's fierce battle, we'll meet
  'mid the combat', said I;
'Can I calm the dark foeman that hates me, with
  love for his child pure and bright?
Can I keep to the promise I made her?' I fled from
  my comrades that night!

VIII.

"I fled like a deer through the mountains, to the
  arms of my Aileen Aroon,—
Oh! great God of glory and mercy, the black fate
  that met me so soon!
She lay in her grave clothes, down-stricken by a
  sickness full sudden and sore,
And my name was the name of traitor, and my
  bright hopes were quenched evermore!

IX.

"From the old pilgrim places around me to gray
  holy Derg of the lake,
Since that wild time of trouble and vengeance, my
  slow yearly pathway I take;
And I pray that my sins be forgiven, by many a
  lone ruined wall,
And I sleep,—but I'll soon sleep beside her, the
  sweetest long slumber of all!"

X.

Oh! mournful stood up the old pilgrim, and mournful took me by the hand:
"May the blessings of love be upon you, and freedom
  and peace in the land!"

Then he drank at the spring in the village, and
   silently went on his way;—
Oh! God and His mercy go with him, a sure prop
   by night and by day!

THE SACK OF DUNBUI.*

A.D. 1602.

I.

They who fell in manhood's pride,
They who nobly fighting died,
  Fade their memories never, never:
    Theirs shall be the deathless name,
    Shining brighter, grander ever
  Up the diamond crags of fame!
Time these glorious names shall lift
Up from sunbright clift to clift,
    Upward! to eternity!
    The godlike men of brave Dunbui!

II.

Glorious men and godlike men,
Well they stemmed the Saxon then,

---

* The Castle of Dunboy or Dunbui, is situated on the shore of Bantry Bay, opposite Beare Island. It belonged to O'Sullivan Beare, and was the great military depot of, and the last fortress that held out for, the Catholics of the South in the year 1602. It was defended, almost successfully, in the summer of that year by 146 men, under their commander, Captain Richard Mac Geoghegan, against an army of nearly 6,000 English, commanded by President Carew. Every man of the 146, together with their heroic commander, fell in its defence, except nine or ten who laid down their arms on condition of their getting quarter, *and were hanged a few minutes afterwards.* Vide *Mac Geoghegan*, and *Annals of the Four Masters*, etc.

When he came with all his powers,
　　Over river, plain, and sea,
　'Gainst the tall and bristling towers
　　　Of the Spartan-manned Dunbui—
Traitor Gael and Saxon churl,
Burning in their wrath to hurl
　　　　Ruin on the bold and free
　　　　Warrior men of brave Dunbui.

III.

Thomond with his traitors came,
Carew breathing blood and flame;
　　First he sent his message in
　　　　To the Southern gunsmen three,
　　Message black as Hell and sin,
　　　　Sin and Satan e'er could be;
Would they trusting freres betray,
Would they this for golden pay?
　　　　Demon, no! foul treachery
　　　　Never dwelt in strong Dunbui.

IV.

Onward then that sunny June,
On they came in the fiery noon,
　　On where frowned the stubborn keep,
　　　　O'er the rock-subduing flood,
　　First they took Beare's island steep,
　　　　And drenched its crags in helpless blood.
Nought could save—child's, woman's tears—
Curse upon their cruel spears!
　　　　Oh, that sight was Hell to see
　　　　By thy bristling walls, Dunbui!

V.

Nearer yet they crowd and come,
With taunting and yelling, and thundering drum,

With taunting and yelling the hold they environ,
　　And swear that its towers and defenders must
　　　　fall,
　While the cannon are set, and their death-hail of
　　　　iron
　　　Crash wildly on bastion and turret and wall;
And the ramparts are torn from their base to their
　　　　brow—
Ho! will they not yield to the murderers now?
　　　　No! its huge towers shall float over Cleena's*
　　　　　　bright sea,
　　　　　Ere the Gael prove a craven in lonely Dun-
　　　　　　bui.

VI.

Like the fierce god of battle Mac Geoghegan goes
From rampart to wall, in the face of his foes;
　Now his voice rises high o'er the cannons' fierce
　　　din,
　　Whilst the taunt of the Saxon is loud as before,
　But a yell thunders up from his warriors within,
　　　And they dash through the gateway, down, down
　　　　to the shore.
With their chief rushing on, like a storm in its wrath,
They sweep the cowed Saxon to death in their path;
　　　Ah! dearly he'll purchase the fall of the free,
　　　Of the lion-souled warriors of lonely Dunbui!

VII.

Leaving terror behind them, and death in their
　　　train,
Now they stand on their walls 'mid the dying and
　　　slain,

---

　* The waters of the Atlantic, south of the shores of Cork.

And the night is around them—the battle is still—
  That lone summer midnight, ah! short is its reign;
For the morn springeth upward, and valley and hill
  Fling back the fierce echoes of conflict again.
And see how the foe rushes up to the breach,
  Towards the green waving banner he yet may not reach,
    For look how the Gael flings him back to the sea,
    From the blood-reeking ramparts of lonely Dunbui!

VIII.

Night cometh again, and the white stars look down
From the hold to the beach, where the batteries frown,
  Night cometh again, but affrighted she flies,
    Like a black Indian queen from the fierce panther's roar,
    And morning leaps up in the wide-spreading skies,
  To his welcome of thunder and flame evermore;
For the guns of the Saxon crash fearfully there,
Till the walls and the towers and the ramparts are bare,
    And the foe make their last mighty swoop on the free,
    The brave-hearted warriors of lonely Dunbui!

IX.

Within the red breach see Mac Geoghegan stand,
  With the blood of the foe on his arm and his brand;

And he turns to his warriors, and "fight we",
    says he,
  "For country, for freedom, religion, and all:
Better sink into death, and for ever be free,
  Than yield to the false Saxon's mercy and thrall!"
And they answer with brandish of sparth and of
    glaive—
"Let them come: we will give them a welcome and
    grave;
    Let them come—from their swords could we
      flinch, could we flee,
    When we fight for our country, our God, and
      Dunbui!"

X.

They came, and the Gael met their merciless shock—
Flung them backward like spray from the lone
    Skellig rock;
  But they rally, as wolves springing up to the
    death
    Of their brother of famine, the bear of the
      snow—
He hurls them adown to the ice-fields beneath,
  Rushing back to his dark norland cave from
    the foe;—
So up to the breaches they savagely bound,
Thousands still thronging beneath and around,
    Till the firm Gael is driven—till the brave
      Gael must flee
    In, into the chambers of lonely Dunbui!

XI.

In chamber, in cellar, on stairway, and tower,
Evermore they resisted the false Saxon's power;

Through the noon, through the eve, and the
    darkness of night
  The clangor of battle rolls fearfully there,
'Till the morning leaps upward in glory and
    light,
    Then, where are the true-hearted warriors of
      Beare?
They have found them a refuge from torment and
  chain:
They have died with their chief, save the few who
  remain,
      And that few—oh, fair Heaven! on the high
        gallows tree
      They swing by the ruins of lonely Dunbui!

XII.

Long, long in the hearts of the brave and the free
Live the warriors who died in the lonely Dunbui—
  Down time's silent river their fair names shall go,
    A light to our race towards the long-coming
      day.;
  Till the billows of time shall be checked in their
    flow
      Can we find names so sweet for remembrance
        as they?
And we will hold their memories for ever and aye,
A halo, a glory that ne'er shall decay,
      We'll set them as stars o'er eternity's sea,
        The bright names of the warriors who fell at
          Dunbui!

THE LADY OF THE SEA.

I.

It was the fairest maiden in Kerry's broad domains,
Her faith did plight to an Irish knight by the shore
    where Cleena reigns;
She was a Saxon maiden—'twas to her father's foe—
And ah, that leal, but hapless love, did cause her
    bitter woe!

II.

For her dark sire had sworn that both their lives
    should be
The forfeit of their meeting by Cleena's murmuring
    sea;
And oft she wept her sister's scorn and her black
    brother's ire,
And oft the stern reproval of her lordly Saxon sire!

III.

She sits beside the greenwood, the lady Jane, alone,
To think upon her hapless love, and make her
    mournful moan;
But grief was gone, and joy soon shone, when by her
    side stood he,
Her banished knight, her Conal Dhuv, the Rover of
    the Sea!

IV.

I've come to thee, my lonely love, back from the
    main sea wave,
An outlawed man, a landless knight, thy hand once
    more to crave:
The grass grows in my castle hall—but fly, my love,
    with me,
And thou shalt reign within my bark, the Lady of
    the Sea!"

V.

Ah! other ears than his have heard the low consent
    she gave
To fly with him next eventide out on the main sea
    wave;
A captain of a pirate bark was lurking in the screen,
And he hath sworn to cross their love—a truthful
    oath I ween.

VI.

It was a golden sunset, a gorgeous eve of May,
And sea and stream beneath the beam in calm
    resplendence lay,
And all alone where towered the crags like giants
    huge and still,
A bonnie page stood pensively by tall Saint Brandon's Hill.

VII.

A belt all bright with ruddy gold was o'er his
    shoulders flung,
A dagger and a silver horn from that glittering belt
    were hung,
And long he gazed upon the deep where sank the
    golden day,
Till round the rock there sudden peered a small
    sail far away.

VIII.

He put the horn unto his mouth, he blew a blast full
    clear,
And to its sound along the waves that light boat
    danced a-near;
But soon he drew his dagger bright—he drew, alas,
    in vain,
For strange dark men around him sprang, and
    forced him o'er the main!

IX.

Scarce vanished was the pirate boat the sunset billows o'er,
When from the sea-beat island crags another sought the shore;
It waited long, it moved a-near, it donned a snow-white sail,
But never sound of bugle horn came whispering on the gale.

X.

At length there leapt upon the strand a youth with eagle eye,
With stately form, and kingly face, and bearing bold and high;
There found the page's blood-stained dirk, and cried, "Ah, woe is me,
Some ruffian band have slain my love, my Lady of the Sea!"

XI.

He rowed his boat full furiously, he gained his bark ere night,
And told the sad tale to his crew in the sunset's waning light.
They sailed away thro' twilight gray, thro' midnight drear and dark,
And when the red morn lit the spray they found the pirate bark.

XII.

An old man stood by Conal Dhuv, his foster-sire was he:
"Now give me speech with yon brave ship, perchance they guiltless be!"

Soon stood he on their deck, and asked for the page
  so young and fine:
"Nor page, nor maid, we've seen", they said, "upon
  the salt sea brine!"

XIII.

The old man looked around their deck: he saw the
  page's horn:
"Now, liars all, mark this!" he cried, with looks of
  hate and scorn;
Then drew his sword and cleared a path, and leapt
  into the sea,
And to his chief despite their shot he swam right
  gallantly!

XIV.

Oh! loud and long the cheer they gave, young
  Conal's gallant crew,
As on the pirate's deck they sprang for vengeance
  stern and true;
Revenge is ta'en, the foe they've slain, though fought
  he fierce and well,
But in that hour of victory their brave young chief-
  tain fell!

XV.

A coronach,* a coronach upon the ocean sheen;
The've brought the lady from the hold, no more a
  page I ween;
They've placed her by her Conal Dhuv, they raise
  the funeral wail,
And ever as they vent their grief they fly before the
  gale.

---

* A *caoine*, or lament.

A coronach, a coronach by Cleena's fairy shore;
The lady died by her lover's side ere th' eve came
    blushing o'er.
A ruin crowns a wave-worn crag; there sweetly
    slumbers he,
Young Donal Dhuv, with his faithful love, his Lady
    of the Sea!

THE DEATH OF O'DONNELL.
A.D. 1257.

I.

Red victory smiled on thy legions, Tir Conaill,
When the Geraldine fell 'neath the sparth* of
    O'Donnel;
But fierce was the wailing, and wild was the sorrow
That broke from thy septs ere the dawn of the
    morrow!
For the prince of their bosoms the champions are
    grieving:
He fell while their axes the fierce foe were cleaving,
And he lies in his death-wounds by Swilly's dark
    river,
With his nation around him, as fearless as ever—
Joy, joy in his heart, tho' its pulses be dying,
That he fell while the foe from his valleys were
    flying.

II.

The clans of Tyrone from their forays returning,
Hear thy death strains, Tir Conaill, and joy in thy
    mourning,

---

* A kind of battle-axe, in the use of which the Irish were peculiarly expert.

That he whose right hand was thy true stay in danger,
Lies wounded to death 'neath the blow of the stranger;
And they well know a nation thus reft of its leader
'Neath the brands of a foe into ruin will speed her.
High hope for O'Niall! How he bands his wild kerne
From the shores of bright Neagh to the green isles of Erne,—
Oh! round him like torrents his vassals come sweeping
Where the waves of strong Derg down the valleys are leaping.

III.

O'Donnell he lies where the green mountain forest
In the glow of the sunlight spreads thickest and hoarest,
While up to his death-couch in frantic disorder
Rush the men of fleet coursers, the scouts of his border;
And they tell in their fear of the black storms looming,
How the red-handed Niall and his thousands are coming!
Then quick spreads the fear of the mighty invader,
Yet all for Tir Conaill are banding to aid her;
And their chieftain—alas! that the death-wounds have bound him—
Calls the men of his might from the valleys around him.

IV.

Then he raises his voice by that wild river billow,
With the gash in his breast and the gore on his pillow—

" O'Niall", he says, " from his mountains of bleakness
Ever came in the hours of our sorrow and weakness:
He pours on our valleys, and now we will greet him
With the welcome of old on the plains where we meet him!
In the day of my strength ye have found me before ye
Where'er your bright claymores to victory bore ye;
In the day of my weakness my soul must be longing
To see how my people to battle are thronging!

V.

Then sound ye, my children, the war note defiant
From the gray Arran cliffs to the Pass of the Giant,
And make me a bier like the biers of my fathers;
Bear me high in your van where the red Niall gathers,*
And we'll scatter his bands, as the storm-clouds of Heaven
From Aileach's black rocks by her thunders are driven!"
Then the hearts of his warriors grow stronger and prouder,
And the shouts of their ardour swell wilder and louder,
And fiercely their war-pipes are ringing and pealing,
From the low-lying glens to the far mountain shieling.

---

* " He then directed his men to place him on the bier which should take him to the grave, and to carry him on it at the head of his forces".—*Haverty's History of Ireland.*— See also *Annals of the Four Masters.*

VI.

They've made him a bier like the biers of his fathers,
They bear him afar where the red Niall gathers—
Six champions of might from that green forest alley
Bear him on thro' each wild glade and torrent-bound valley,
To a small mountain plain by a swift river torn,
Where the May-heather gleams in the dew of the morn;
But its vernal expanse by the fairy-rings spotted,
Ere the sheen of the evening with gore shall be clotted,
For there with their claymores so gallantly flashing
The septs of Tyrone on Tir Conaill are dashing!

VII.

Oh, fiercely they meet! As the foam-wreathed surges,
When some demon of midnight their black fury urges
To shatter thy cross, Ard Oilean of the prayers,
So rush and so meet the wild bands of the slayers!
Soon the septs of Tyrone in their might are prevailing,
And the strength of Tir Conaill is riven and failing—
But the bier! the black bier! with the prince of their valour,—
Oh! they look on his face in its last mortal pallor,
And they band them once more and rush fiercely together
On the files of Tyrone o'er the blood-crimsoned heather.

VIII.

Shout, shout for Tir Conaill! Hurra! for her striving!
Now the ranks of the foeman her claymores are riving;
The hoofs of her steeds through his red blood are plashing,
And each rider's bright sparth 'mid his squadrons is crashing!
As a herd of gray wolves the O'Niall she scatters,
As the dust of the desert his legions she shatters;
But who in her next hour of need will defend her?
For a corse on his bier lies the prince of her splendour!
Oh! he died while his flags waved in victory o'er him,
With the last of his foemen far scattered before him!

IX.

He worsted the stranger, he routed O'Niall,
And long, long again ere they band for the trial;
Too well they remember the welcome he gave them,
When flight, nor the strength of their numbers could save them.
Oh! loud through the wild hills his coronach swelleth,
It startles the dun deer and wolf where he dwelleth;
There are eyes red with sorrow, from Erne's green islands
To wild Inishone of the wood-belted highlands;
For they'll ne'er meet his peer in the sad hour of danger
'Gainst the septs of the south, or the false-hearted stranger!

MARY'S SWEETHEART.

I.

The first time that I saw my love, I knew his heart was mine,
The next time that I saw my love, I thought he was divine;*
For he said he was no rover, and would ne'er leave me to pine,
And oh! my heart is happy with this true-love of mine!

II.

I met him at the Patron by Saint Molagga's Tree,
Where at the dance and hurling the boldest, best was he;
Oh! my heart was very happy on that blissful holiday,
And I learned to love him dearly while we danced the hours away.

III.

My Brian Ban is clothed in garments of the frieze;
But 'tis not costly garments or hoarded wealth I prize;
'Tis the truthful heart he gave me, 'tis the glance of his kind eyes,
And the loving tales he tells me while the golden daylight dies!

IV.

A brave heart's in his bosom, yet he's gentle as a child:
He tells me pleasant stories till with laughter I am wild;

---

* The first two lines belong to an old song sung in Munster.

He'll ofttimes change to sadness, and make me sob
    and cry,
Then kiss my bitter tears away, till none so glad
    as I!

V.

Oh! he was scarce a stripling when he banded with
    the men
That wanted Ireland's freedom, but could not get it
    then;
And long a gallant outlaw he kept the mountain
    glen;
But for old Ireland's freedom he'd venture more
    again.

VI.

And now he sits beside me in the greenest dell of
    dells,
And the sweetest of all stories my fond, fond dar-
    ling tells,
That he loves me with a constant love, that never
    can decay,
Till we sleep beneath the green grass in Molagga's
    churchyard gray!

VII.

On lands and money hoarded my father sets great
    store,
Though 'gainst the poor and needy he never shut his
    door;
But my Brian owns a ploughland, and my father
    asks no more,
So we are to be married when the Easter days are
    o'er!

TYRRELL'S PASS.
A.D. 1579.

I.

By the flowery banks of Inny the burning sunset fell,
In many a stream and golden gleam on hill and mead
    and dell,
And from thy shores, bright Ennel, to the far-off
    mountain crest,
O'er plain and leafy wildwood there was peace and
    quiet rest.
Oh! sunset is the sweetest of all the hours that be
For musing lone, or tale of love, by glen or forest
    tree;
But its radiance bringeth saddening thoughts to him
    whose good right hand
Must guard his life in the coming strife 'gainst the
    foe of his fatherland;
For he knows when thinking lonely by his small tent
    on the plain
The glories of the sinking sun he ne'er may see again!

II.

Brave Tyrrell sat that summer eve amid the forest
    hills
With Captain Owen at his side, by Inny's fountain
    rills—
Brave Tyrrell of the flying camps, and Owen Oge
    of Cong—
And round them lay their warriors wild the forest
    glade along.
Four hundred men of proof they were, these warriors
    free and bold;
In many a group they sat around the green skirts of
    the wold;

Some telling of their early loves, and some of mighty deeds,
In regions wide by Shannon side, in Galien of the steeds—
Some cursing the Invader's steps, and wishing for the fray,
That they might sate their burning hate ere the close of that bright day.

III.

Ah! well and deeply they might hate the dark Invader then;
His steps were seen in valley green, in fertile plain and glen;
The gory field, the rifled town, the hamlet burned and lone,—
These were the marks by which he made his demon footsteps known!
He came with all his legions in their new-made light and zeal,—
He came with robber heart and hand and with the murderer's steel;
He came to root the ancient faith from out their native land,
And plant his godless temples where her fanes were wont to stand—
He came to sweep their race away, in hatred hot and keen,
That future lands might never know where such a race had been!

IV.

The sun had set upon their camp, the stars were burning bright,
All, save the chief and Owen Oge, were sleeping in their light;

And they sat downward where the stream was
    singing its deep song,
Planning fierce raid and foray bold that starry
    twilight long.
"By my good faith", said Tyrrell, "we have wan-
    dered far and wide,
And on no foe, still, high or low, our good swords
    have we tried;
There's many a keep around us here, and many a
    traitor town,
And we will have a town, or keep, before two suns
    go down!"
Said Owen Oge, "No! Heaven send our banded foe-
    men here,
A pleasant fight in the cool of night, 'neath the star-
    light still and clear!"—

v.

With flashing sabres to their feet both warriors
    instant sprang,
And down the little streamlet's bed their challenge
    fiercely rang!—
They'd heard a sound beside the stream, as if some
    forest bird,
Awakening from his twilight dreams amid the leaves
    had stirred;
Another stir like the stealthy step of a wolf from out
    his lair,
And their trusty spy of the falcon eye stood right
    before them there!
"The foe, with baron Trimblestown high boasting
    at their head,
Will find ye here in these green glades at morning
    light", he said,
Then vanished silent as he came beneath the forest
    shade,
And the clank of sabres followed him on his pathway
    through the glade.

VI.

For his comrades at their leader's call beside the
    streamlet's bank
Were filing from their ferny beds in many a serried
    rank,
And now along their ordered lines Fertullagh's
    accents came—
"The foeman o'er our native fields speeds down with
    sword and flame,
We'll meet him as we ever met—the same red wel-
    come still—
We'll meet him in the eastward pass, and sweep him
    from the hill!"
They gained that pass ere morning leapt above the
    eastern wave,
And half his band to Owen Oge the hardy chieftain
    gave—
"Now lie ye here in ambush close till we may turn
    below,
And when ye hear my trumpet call, spring out upon
    the foe!"

VII.

There came no sound from that deep pass—e'en
    from the mountain fern
No deep breath of the gallowglass, or whispering of
    the kern—
No sounding, save the raven's voice around the
    jutting crags,
Hoarse croaking for the morrow's feast upon their
    flinty jags.
And now along the mist-clad hills out shone the
    morning ray
On Barnwell's bright and serried files all burning
    for the fray—

Eight hundred men of might they were from fat
 Meath's fertile plain,
And when they saw Fertullagh's men they laughed
 in high disdain—
"Two hundred men to stem our charge! We'll
 chase them till they stand!"
Then poured them in to that deep glynn upon the
 flying band.

VIII.

Now Tyrrell wheels his warriors round, out rings his
 trumpet note,
'Tis answered by the drum's deep sound from the
 gorge's hollow throat—
The frighted wolf leaps up the hill—"Ha! ha!" the
 ravens shriek,
"We'll soon have food for each famished brood—
 rider and war-horse sleek!"—
And down like pards from their forest glades on a
 herd of startled deer,
The brave four hundred fiercely rush on the foeman's van and rere!
The kerne go darting in the first with their guns
 and gleaming pikes—
Ah! woe the day for the struggling foe where'er
 that weapon strikes—
The giant gallowglass strides down with vengeance
 in his eye,
Wild yelling out his charging shout like a thunder-
 clap on high!

IX.

Now up the woody mountain side the battle rolls
 along;
Now down into the valley's womb the tugging
 warriors throng—

As hounds around a hunted wolf some forest rock
  beneath,
Whence comes no sound save the mortal rush and
  the gnash of many teeth,
Their charging shouts have died away—no sound
  rolls upwards save
The volley of the murderous gun, and the crash of
  axe and glaive!
Oh! life it is a precious gem, yet many there will
  throw
The gem away in that mortal fray for vengeance on
  their foe,
And thus they tug more silent still, till the glen is
  covered wide
With war-steed strong, and sabred corse, and many
  a gory tide.

x.

Hurrah! that shout it rolleth up with cadence wild
  and stern!
'Tis the triumph roar of the gallowglass, and the
  sharp yell of the kern;
The foeman flies before their steel—not far, not far
  he flies;
In the gorge's mouth, in the valley's womb, by the
  mountain foot he dies;
Where'er he speeds, death follows him like a shadow
  in his tracks—
He meets the gleam of the fearful pike, and the
  sharp and gory axe!
Their leader of the boasting words, young Trimblestown, was ta'en,
And his champions all, save one weak man, in that
  bloody gorge were slain—
They speed him on unchased by kern, unsmote by
  gallowglass,
That he might tell how his comrades fell that morn
  in Tyrrell's Pass!

THE BATTLE OF THE RAVEN'S GLEN.*

A.D. 1603.

I.

From his turrets that look to the silver Kinmera,
From the halls of his splendour by Bantry and
    Bearra,
With his band of brave warriors, O'Sullivan bore
    him—
Till the mountains of Limerick rose darkly before
    him;
There he camped 'mid the rocks, where the deep
    pools were paven
By the white stars of night, in the glen of the
    Raven!

II.

In that glen was no sound, save the murmur of
    fountains,
And the moonbeams were silvering the thunder-
    split mountains,
When a horse-tramp rang wildly from Ounanar's
    water,
Rolling up from the gorge of the dark Vale of
    Slaughter,

---

* O'Sullivan, Prince of Bearre and Bantry, during his flight to Tyrone, in the winter of 1603, was attacked by the De Barrys of Buttevant, with the septs of the surrounding baronies, in the mountains of Ballagh Abhra, now Bally-houra. He defeated them with great slaughter, as he did all that came in his way during that memorable flight, and encamped for three days and nights in the scene of the battle, the Raven's Glen, near the old church of Ardpatrick.

And the rider ne'er reined till his long plume was waven
By the breezes that sighed thro' the Glen of the Raven!

III.

Up sprang to their saddles the chieftains around him,
And they asked where the foe 'mid the forests had found him;
For they knew he had passed thro' the battle's fierce labour,
From the foam o'er his steed and the blood on his sabre—
While the rocks with the hoofs of their chargers were graven,
As they pranced into lines 'mid the Glen of the Raven!

IV.

'Twas the scout of lone Bregog: he'd heard in the gloaming
Fierce yells o'er that wild torrent's thunder and foaming,
Then a dash, and a roar, and a rushing did follow,
For the foe burst around him from moorland and hollow,
But a road to his chief thro' their ranks he had claven—
Now he stood by his side in the Glen of the Raven!

V.

Up started Black Hugh from his couch in the fern—
The outlaw of Dara, and Brona the stern—

"There's a passage", he said, "over Ounanar's water,*
Where Clan Morna of old were defeated with slaughter;
There bide we the steps of the traitor and craven—
And he ne'er shall come down thro' the Glen of the Raven!"

VI.

The ambush was set in the Passage of Lightning,
And now in the moonlight, sharp weapons came bright'ning,
The lance of the Saxon, from Mulla and Mallow,
And the pike of the kern, from the wilds of Duhallow—
Soon they clashed with the swords of the men of Berehaven,
Till the echoes rolled back through the Glen of the Raven!

VII.

But back was the ambush now scattered and driven—
Yet the ranks of their foe were as fearfully riven!
And onward, and round them, the foemen came pouring,
With the wild torrent's speed, and its strength and its roaring,

---

* There is a tradition that the Clan Morna were defeated here by the Clan Baskin; hence the name of the glen—Glenanar, or the Valley of Slaughter. There is a ford across this glen, near its upper extremity, called Aha Suillish, or the Ford of the Light. Mulla, the Aubeg, a beautiful stream flowing by Buttevant and Doneraile.

Till the ambush were swept where the Druid had graven
His god on the crags, by the Glen of the Raven!

VIII.

Then O'Sullivan burst like the angel of slaughter,
By the dark rushing current of Geerath's wild water,
And the brave men of Cork, and of Kerry's wild regions,
Were his rushing destroyers, his death-dealing legions—
And onward they rode over traitor and craven,—
Whose bones long bestrewed the lone Glen of the Raven!

IX.

All silent again over forest and mountain,
Save the voice in that gorge of Oiseen's ancient fountain;
While O'Sullivan's crest, with its proud eagle feather,
And broadswords and pikes, glitter now from the heather;
For where the dark pools with the white stars are paven,
Secure rests the clan in the Glen of the Raven!

SONGS.

MY BOAT.

Air—" I'll build my love a gallant ship".

I.

My boat is like the seagull white
    That skims o'er strand and swell,
It looks so bright and sails so light,
    And stems the tide so well;
The soft wild gale fills out its sail
    And wafts it towards the sea,
And floats me down from Cork's fair town
    Upon the pleasant Lee.

II.

I sit within that bonnie boat
    When love o'er me has power,
When sea birds float with shrilly note
    At sunset's golden hour;
Then from the shore green towering o'er
    Love seems to pilot me,
To muse alone on my loved one
    Upon the pleasant Lee.

III.

When first my boat upon the tide
    A thing of life out came,
With conscious pride upon its side
    I placed my true-love's name;

And since, each day, that name the spray
   Has washed full wild and free,
But still each line undimmed doth shine,
   Upon the pleasant Lee.

IV.

A trim new sail my boat shall have
   When summer days come on,
And swift and brave she'll walk the wave,
   More stately than the swan;
For then my bloom-bright maid shall come
   With love and joy to me,
And side by side we oft shall glide
   Upon the pleasant Lee.

THE MOUNTAINS HIGH.

Air—"'Tis with my gun I'll guard you".

I.

On lowland plains I wander
   All in the falling year,
By lowland valleys ponder
   Upon my true-love dear;
But spring will soon restore me
   The smiles of Mary's eye,
And the grand clouds flying o'er me
   Upon the mountains high.

II.

Within the lowland valley
   There stands a castle strong,
Where round in each green alley
   You'll hear the wild bird's song;

Far sweeter visions move me,
　　When I hear the eagle's cry
From the fields of God above me,
　　Upon the mountains high.

III.

When autumn time is coming
　　Along the hills and dells,
You'll hear the wild bees humming
　　Among the heather bells;
You'll hear the gay streams singing
　　Their songs to earth and sky,
Like the sounds of glad bells ringing
　　Upon the mountains high.

IV.

Amid their summits airy,
　　In sweet spring's blessed reign,
I'll sit beside my Mary
　　With happy heart again;
I have no wish beyond her,
　　And man can ne'er descry
Two youthful lovers fonder
　　Upon the mountains high.

WILL OF THE GAP.

Air—"Graine Weal".

I.

In castle or town was there never a man
Could handle a broadsword or empty a can,
Could glory in danger, whatever might hap,
Like the Outlaw of Sloragh, young Will of the Gap!

II.

From his boot to his basnet was burnished so sheen,
And his arm was so strong, and his sword was so keen;
And his brain was the brightest that e'er laid a trap
To catch the proud Saxon—young Will of the Gap.

III.

Up rose in the morning the Ridderah Fionn,*
And spurred with his vassals by forest and down,
To catch Will asleep in the mountain's broad lap;
But the sleep of a fox slept young Will of the Gap!

IV.

For he'd gathered his men ere the Ridderah knew,
And he placed them in ambush by lone Rossarue:
"Now he thinks he will catch us just taking our nap,
But we'll open *his* eyes!" said young Will of the Gap.

V.

The Ridderah rode with his wild vassals in,
Till he reached the deep bosom of Rossa's lone glynn;—
"Now the Ridderah's caught in his own wily trap,
So blow up the trumpet!" cried Will of the Gap.

VI.

The signal was blown, and the ambush behind
And the ambush before thundered down like the wind,
And scarcely three vassals, to tell their mishap,
With the White Knight 'scaped free from young Will of the Gap!

---

* Ridderah Fionn, the White Knight, lord of Kilbenny.

MY HEART IS WILD.

Air—"I travelled this country".

I.

My heart is wild with the love I bear
For my maiden mild of the yellow hair,
Of the yellow hair and the low, fond sighs,
Of the form so fair and the star-bright eyes.

II.

I know a tree in a distant glade,
And it mindeth me of my own dear maid;
Where'er I strayed was no fairer tree,
No fairer maid than my love to me.

III.

In a fairy dell by the moorland height
I know a well, calm, pure, and bright:
In its waves of light the sunbeams play,
Like the glances bright of my lovely May.

IV.

By the gentle hill, and gray rock piled,
Leaps down that rill like a gladsome child—
Oh! my heart's as wild with the love I bear
For my maiden mild of the yellow hair.

THE FLOWER THAT NE'ER SHALL FADE.

Air—" The doctor tries all remedies".

I.

The primrose and the woodbine bower
　By streams their fragrance fling,
And sweetly blooms the Drinan flower
　Amid the dells in spring;

The red, red rose full brightly blows
    In many a garden shade;
But flowers and blooms, when winter comes,
    All darkly die and fade.

II.

I know a flower that ne'er shall die,
    More dear than life to me,—
In Mary's heart that flower doth lie
    Of love and constancy;
The blooms may go, when winter's snow
    Robes hill and greenwood glade,
And storms may lower, but oh! that flower
    Shall never die or fade.

THE CANNON.

Air—"Barrack Hill".

I.

We are a loving company
    Of soldiers brave and hearty;
We never fought for golden fee,
    For faction, or for party;—
The will to make old Ireland free,
    That set each dauntless man on,
Which banished us beyond the sea,
    With our brave iron cannon
        And here's the gallant company
            That fought by Boyne and Shannon,
        That never feared an enemy,
            With our brave iron cannon!

II.

Come fill me up a pint of wine,
    Until 'tis brimming o'er, boys,
Our gun is set in proper line,
    And we have balls galore, boys,—

Now here's a health to good Lord Clare,
  Who'll lead us on to-morrow,
When through the foe our balls will tear,
  And work them death and sorrow!
    And here's the gallant company
      That always forward ran on
    So boldly on the enemy,
      With our brave iron cannon!

III.

I've brought a wreath of shamrocks here,
  In memory of our own land—
'Tis withered like that island drear,—
  That sorrowful and lone land;
I'll hang it nigh our cannon's mouth,
  To whet our memories fairly,
And there's no flower in all the south
  Could deck that gun so rarely!
    And here's the gallant company
      That soon shall rush each man on,
    And plough the Saxon enemy
      With our brave iron cannon!

IV.

At Limerick how it made them run,
  The Dutchman and his crew, boys;
'Twas then I made this gallant gun
  To plough them through and through, boys;
And since that day in foreign lands
  It roared triumphant ever—
It blazed away, yet here it stands,
  Where foeman's foot shall never!
    And here's the gallant company
      That soon shall rush each man on,
    And break and strew the enemy
      With our brave iron cannon!

V.

'Tis dinted well from mouth to breech
    With many a battle furrow;
A fitting sermon it will preach
    At Fontenoy to-morrow.
Then never let your spirits sink,
    But stand around, each man on
This foreign slope, and we will drink
    One brave health to our cannon!
        And here's the gallant company
            That soon shall rush each man on,
        And plough the Saxon enemy
            With our brave iron cannon!

THE STUDENT.

Air—"Oh! may I marry thee?"

I.

The live-long day, and many a night,
    Upon my books I pore,
And is it all for fame's delight,
    Or all for golden store?
It is not for the golden pay,
    Or fame's bright face to see,
But oh! to hurry on the day
    When I may marry thee,
        My love,
When I may marry thee.

II.

The breezy morn, the sunset bright,
    To me no gladness bring,
Nor summer with its bloom and light,
    Nor freshness of the spring;—

Yet I have glimpses of a ray
　　　　As bright as they can be—
　　Thy fond look on that happy day
　　　　When I may marry thee,
　　　　　　　　My love,
　　　When I may marry thee.

III.

I thought to seek a soldier's lot,—
　　Bright fame, or narrow bed,—
Yet I am chained to one lone spot,
　　By love-hopes only led;
But heart and brain shall win their way
　　To some good destiny,
And hurry on the blissful day,
　　When I may marry thee,
　　　　　　My love,
　　When I may marry thee.

MY STEED WAS WEARY.

Air—"'Twas early, early all in the spring".

I.

My steed was weary upon the hill,
While the night came down and the winds blew chill;
But I thought of thee by the distant Nore,
And my heart was nerved for the way once more.

II.

My steed was weary beside the wood,
And I knew his weakness to swim the flood;
But I thought of thee by the distant Nore,
And I spurred him safe to the other shore.

III.

My steed was weary beside the fen;
He saw the danger, and feared it then;
But I thought of thee by the distant Nore,
And safely, safely, I brought him o'er.

IV.

My steed dropt down by the mountain lake,
And I slept by his side in the wild ash brake,
And I dreamt of thee by the distant Nore,
Till the morning's splendours came shining o'er.

V.

Then up I stood with my steed again,
And I reached my home in the lowland plain,
And my thoughts of thee by the distant Nore
Were sweeter and brighter than e'er before.

FAR AWAY.

Air—"I might have got an earl".

I.

Along the winding river
  The wintry tempests blow;
The sere leaves glance and quiver
  Within the wave below;
The sun is redly sinking
  Beyond the mountains gray,
And I am ever thinking
  Of her that's far away.

II.

Her eyes are like the vi'lets
  In some green summer dell;
The rose of Lene's bright islets
  Her lips can ne'er excel—

That wild lake of the mountain,
  Its depths no man can say;
My love's as deep a fountain
  For her that's far away.

III.

Oh! were I like the earls
  That reigned o'er Desmond's towers,
Her hair should shine with pearls,
  Instead of fading flowers,
And robes of queenly splendour
  Her fair form should array,
My love's so true and tender
  For her that's far away.

IV.

Oh! could you see her golden
  Bright locks, and form so fine,
You'd think some goddess olden
  Had witched those eyes of thine;
And while the sun is sinking,
  I'm spell-bound day by day,
For oh! I'm ever thinking
  Of her that's far away.

THE MOUNTAIN ASH.

Air—"The Green Ash Tree".

I.

The mountain ash blooms in the wild,
  Or droops above the wandering rill;
    You ne'er can see
    A fairer tree,
But I know one dear maiden mild
  With witching form more lovely still.

II.

The mountain ash has berries fair,
  The reddest in the woodlands green;
    Sweet lips I know
    With redder glow
Than ever lit those berries rare—
  The red lips of my bosom's queen.

III.

The mountain ash has leaves of gold,
  When autumn browns the steep hill's side:
    Of locks I dream
    With brighter gleam
Of yellow in their braid and fold
  Than e'er tinged leaf in woodland wide.

IV.

The mountain ash in winter sere
  Stands bravely up when wild winds blow;
    So love shall stand,
    Serene and bland,
Between me and my Ellen dear,
  A fadeless flower in weal or woe.

THE ENSIGN AND HIS BANNER.

A BRIGADE SONG.

Air—"The Green Flag".

I.

They said I was too young to seek
  For fame or martial glory;
They said I was too slight and weak
  To brave the battle gory;

But years have passed, and I have got
    A soldier's mien and manner,
And borne thro' many a storm of shot
    My conquering Irish banner.

II.

The bloody breach of strong Namur,
    It was the first I mounted,
And many a comrade's corse be sure
    Within that breach we counted;
There placed we high the *Fleur de lys*,
    And Bill,* th' old Dutch trepanner,
As fast he fled, looked back on thee,
    Far higher still, my banner!

III.

And since that mighty day of death,
    With honour still I've borne it:
It waved in many a battle's breath,
    And many a shot has torn it:
It saw on Steinkirk's fiery plain
    Brave Sarsfield beat the planner
Of all our woe, Dutch Bill, again,
    My glorious Irish banner.

IV.

I had a sweetheart in Ireland
    Before I crossed the water:
My comrades say some Saxon band
    Has drenched her home in slaughter;
Ah! cold she sleeps—God rest her soul!—
    Beside the Banks of Anner,
And now I've nought, as seasons roll,
    To love, but my green banner!

---

* Dutch Bill, the name by which King William is almost universally known in the south of Ireland.

V.

And now where'er my banner wave,
  I'll think on that sad river,
Where lies my true love's gory grave,
  And fight for vengeance ever;—
With Ireland's woes in memory,
  Some brave revenge I'll plan her,
And when I fall, my shroud shall be
  My glorious Irish banner!

I NEVER CAN FORGET.

Air—" I can't forget".

I.

My Mary said to me
  That she loved but me alone,
And oh! how gladsomely
  I heard that kind word's tone;
She said she'd give her life
  For me without regret;
She said she'd be my wife—
  Can I these words forget?
    Oh! glad they make me yet,
    Within my fond heart set,—
    The memory of that happy hour
    I never can forget.

II.

My Mary dwells beside
  The glancing, dancing Nore,
Where it flings its sparkling tide
  From the mountains high and hoar;

She's a fair, bright lady born—
  None fairer in the land;
And she pledged to me one morn
  Her loving heart and hand.
    Oh! glad it makes me yet,
    Within my fond heart set,—
    The memory of that happy hour
    I never can forget.

III.

It was too soon to part,
  But soon again we'll meet,
When I'll clasp her to my heart
  And worship at her feet;
Oh! fondly, fondly there
  My vows again I'll pour,
When the flowers are springing fair
  By the glancing, dancing Nore!
    Oh! glad it makes me yet,
    Within my fond heart set,—
    The memory of that happy hour
    I never can forget.

THE COCK AND THE SPARROW.

Air—"The Game Cock".

I.

One morn at the sack of Cragnour,
  A cock and a sparrow were speaking,
While 'neath where they sat on the tower
  The crop-ears their fury were wreaking—
Were wreaking in blood, fire, and smoke—
  "Ah! the castle is ta'en, bone and marrow,
And my poor Irish heart it is broke!"
  Said the brave jolly cock to the sparrow.

II.

" For the crop-ears will have us full soon,
  And our bed will be no bed of roses:
They will starve us right dead to the tune
  Of a psalm that they'll twang thro' their noses;
Never more shall I crow in the hall,
  For the gloom there my bosom would harrow—
May the fiend whip them off, psalms and all!"
  Said the brave jolly cock to the sparrow.

III.

" 'Tis certain the castle they've got,
  And 'tis sure that they'll slay all that's in it;
But as victory is theirs, and what not,
  You're expected to crow like a linnet!"
Cried the sparrow, with voice sad and low:—
  But " I'd rather my grave cold and narrow,
Than at Puritan triumph to crow!"
  Said the brave jolly cock to the sparrow.

IV.

" No more", said the sparrow, " we'll see
  Irish gallants come in late and early;
No more shall they hunt o'er the lea,
  When the sweet autumn wind shakes the barley;
Never more shall they dance on the bawn,
  Or ride from the gate like an arrow!"—
" Ah! no more shall I wake them at dawn!"
  Said the brave jolly cock to the sparrow.

V.

But the chief of Cragnour soon returned,
  And the crop-ears right sorely he hammered;
Then the sparrow with gleefulness burned,
  And " Hurra for my Irish!" he clamoured;—

And " Hurra for the chief of Cragnour!
    There is joy through my flesh, bone, and marrow,
For his vict'ry I'll crow hour by hour!"
    Said the brave jolly cock to the sparrow!

THERE IS A STREAM.

Air—" As I was riding out one day".

I.

There is a stream mid Houra's dells
    That dances downward fleetly,
That mirrors rocks and heather-bells
    And sings by wild woods sweetly,
With drooping birch and Drinan Dhun
    Its vernal banks adorning,—
And there my love with sweet smiles won
    My fond heart in the morning.

II.

God bless the May that brought to me
    The love that nought can sunder!
God bless the odorous Drinan tree,
    That we sat fondly under!
The skies were blue, the clouds were bright,
    The valleys shade and splendour,
And Annie's eyes were filled with light
    Of love all true and tender.

III.

And oft within that valley lone
    We met on May-days after,
While aye the stream went murmuring on
    With sounds like fairy laughter;
'Tis there a rill, but far below
    It winds, a calm bright river,—
Thus may our firm love forward go,
    Increasing on for ever!

DONAL O'KEEFFE'S LAMENT.

Air—" She's a dear maid to me".

I.

My name is Donal Dhu—an Outlaw bold and true,
    I ranged the country thro', from Saxon bondage free,
Till I loved a maiden fair, with her glossy curling hair,
    But she sunk me in despair—she's a dear maid to me!

II.

My sires were princes grand within old Ireland's land:
    With many a knightly band they held their castles free,
Till the Saxon with them strove—an outlaw now I rove,
    Lamenting my false love—she's a dear maid to me!

III.

Her brow like wintry snows, her cheeks were like the rose
    That nigh Blackwater blows when summer decks the tree;
Her dark eyes glittered bright, full, full of love's delight,—
    They haunt me day and night—she's a dear maid to me!

IV.

With gems of costly sheen I decked my mountain queen,
  And glorious was her mien of beauty fresh and free;
Her step was like the fawn on Araglin's wild lawn,
  Her smile was like the dawn—she's a dear maid to me!

V.

Margaret Kelly was her name, and burning was the flame
  That o'er our bosoms came when we first loved trustingly,
But her love grew false and cold, and her outlaw's life she sold
  For the Saxon's worthless gold—she's a dear maid to me!

VI.

Oh! woeful was the hour that revenge o'er me had power
  To slay my beauteous flower, when I knew her perfidy—
I drew my skian unblest, and with rage and grief possest,
  I plunged it in her breast—she's a dear maid to me!

VII.

And now I've 'scaped the chain, and now I'm free again,
  On many a battle plain I will let the Saxons see
What their traitor wiles shall prove, tho' an outlaw still I rove,
  Lamenting my false love—she's a dear maid to me

I THOUGHT SHE LOVED ME DEARLY.

Air—"Oh! why are you false?"

I.

I was up in the morning early
　With a heart from sorrow clear,
For I thought she loved me dearly
　In the spring-time of the year:
That my Eileen loved me dearly
　In the spring-time of the year.

II.

I climbed up the mountains cheer'ly;
　But long that morn I'll rue,
For she said she loved me dearly,
　And I found her all untrue:
On that summer morning early
　My Eileen Bán untrue!

III.

Her love oped sweet and clearly,
　Like the bloom of the wild rose tree;
But a false wind stirred it drearly,
　And 'tis withered and dead to me;
It blew o'er her heart so drearly,
　And blighted her love for me.

IV.

Ah! Eileen, how sincerely
　My heart aye beat for thee,—
You said you loved me dearly,
　And why prove false to me?
In the summer of love so early,
　Oh! why prove false to me?

THE MERRY CHRISTMAS FIRE.

Air—"The first night I was married".

I.

In summer time my heart is glad,
    In autumn low or gay,
But there is sweet, and nought of sad,
    When Christmas comes alway;
And never bliss more sweet than this
    Can happy man desire,
Than sit a-near his true love dear
    By the merry Christmas fire.

II.

In summer time the vales are bright
    With glancing leaf and flower,
And autumn spreads its amber light
    On many a lovely bower;
And sweetly sing the birds in spring,
    Like tune of fairy lyre;
But far more dear, my true love near,
    And the merry Christmas fire.

III.

From the Christmas fire the gay flames dart,
    And glance, and glow, and whirl,
Like the fire of love within my heart
    For my own sweet Irish girl.
Oh! gladdest boon to sit full soon,
    Where young heart ne'er could tire,
All fondly near my true love dear,
    By the merry Christmas fire.

MY TRUE LOVE BRIGHT.

Air—" The summer is come".

I.

The winds were stayed in their endless flight,
O'er storied valley and mountain height,
As I sat me down with a wild delight
To think an hour on my true love bright.

II.

My true love bright dwells far away;
My true love hears not her minstrel's lay;
Yet I know, oh! I know that she ne'er will stray
From the love she plighted that winter day.

III.

The glittering stars that hang on high
Have beams like the beams of my true love's eye;
When I speak to my love, her words reply
Like an angel's song in the crystal sky.

IV.

The lily flower by the wave-lit strand
Is white, like the white of my true love's hand,
And a rose doth smile in some golden land
Like the smiles of my love so sweet and bland.

V.

In Paradise by a blest stream's shore,
The amaranth bloometh for evermore;
That flower will wither and die before
I cease to love, or my maid adore.

VI.

And golden noon and starred midnight
Go my thoughts to her, like the fleet wind's flight;
For evermore with a wild delight
I fondly think on my true love bright.

THE RED LUSMORE.

Air—"The blooming meadow".

I.

The snow is on the mountains high,
    The bloom has left the heather,
But laughing spring will soon be nigh,
    And summer's golden weather;
Then many a vale we'll wander o'er,
    Whose streams leap glad and fleetly,
And many a glen of red lusmore*
    That shines in June so sweetly.

II.

What makes me love the lusmores gay,
    With all their bright bells round them?
My dear one's lips are red as they,
    And sweet as bee e'er found them;
And oh! it shines by torrents hoar,
    In haunts of sprite and fairy,
Where many an hour in days of yore,
    I dreamt of one like Mary.

---

* *Lusmore*, i.e., the great herb—the Foxglove.

III.

While purple decks its gorgeous bells
    I'll never seek a new love;
In summer time, where'er it dwells,
    I'll wander with my true love;
And aye I'll kiss her o'er and o'er,
    And vow my fond vows meetly,
In fairy glens of red lusmore,
    That shines in June so sweetly.

GRA GAL MACHREE.

Air—"Ne'er wed an old man".

I.

When morning discloses its light on the roses
    Upon them reposes the sweet honey dew;
Like buds of their fairest, thy lips, oh! my dearest,
    Have honey the rarest to sweeten them too;
Thine eyes they are brighter than stars of the night, or
    Than April skies' light, or than gems of the sea;
Thy neck's like th' illuming bright lily assuming
    Its first tender blooming, sweet Gra Gal Machree.

II.

I went to the greenwood that streamlets serene would
    Make music, and sheen, would enliven me more:
Sweet visions they wrought me, sweet mem'ries they brought me,
    Of thee, who first taught me love's passion and lore;

The birds round me winging, their carols were
    singing,
  Their voices outringing with rapture and glee;
My heart then enchanted, by dearer tones haunted,
  For thy loved words panted, sweet Gra Gal Machree.

III.

O Love! I am thinking of thee, from the blinking
  Of morn till the sinking of day in the west,
And thus each fair creature and bright blooming
    feature
  And aspect of nature brings joy to my breast;
Each night through the airy sweet dreamland of fairy
  My soul still unweary is wand'ring to thee,
And dream, or reflection, is one recollection
  Of thy fond affection, sweet Gra Gal Machree.

ALONG WITH MY LOVE I'LL GO.

Air—"The roads they are wet and wintry, love".

I.

My love has an eye of brightness,
    An arm of valour free;
My love has a heart of lightness,
    But ever true to me;—
The pride of my heart unchanging,
    His black locks' martial flow,
And away to the wild wars ranging,
    Along with my love I'll go.

II.

They tell me of the strangers
    Who waste our island fair,
That war has toils and dangers
    Too stern for me to bear,—

The stranger's gory rieving
  May lay our dwellings low;
Yet to my fond troth cleaving,
  Along with my love I'll go.

III.

The woods wear winter sadness,
  White falls the icy shower,
There's shelter, peace, and gladness
  Within my father's tower,—
I bore the summer's burning,
  I heed not winter's snow,
And thus through joy or mourning
  Along with my love I'll go.

IV.

Oh! ne'er for once to leave him
  In tented field or hall,
To smile if joy receive him,
  Or die if he should fall;
And ever thus unchanging,
  Thro' want, and toil, and woe,
Away to the wild wars ranging
  Along with my love I'll go.

THE SPRING OF THE YEAR.

Air—"The Spring of the Year".

I.

We sat by the verge of the forest,
  Where flowers shone like stars in the ray,
Where steep rocks towered highest and hoarest,
  'Mid those hills of the east far away;

And sweet was the fond love that bound us,
   Undimmed by all doubting and fear,
And young like the fresh flowers around us,
   In the soft blooming spring of the year.

II.

The breeze brushed the stream into splendour,
   And murmured down valley and lea;
The wild birds sang songs low and tender
   To none but my darling and me;
And sweet were the smiles of my true love,
   And bright were the eyes of my dear,
A-sparkling with warm rays of new love
   In the soft blooming spring of the year.

III.

The bronzed nuts in autumn that cluster,
   The golden-leaved sprays drooping down,
Are dim near the amber-bright lustre
   That gleamed in her long locks of brown;
Her cheeks like the rose of the morning,
   Her neck like the blooms of the brere,
That smile, all the woodlands adorning,
   In the soft blooming spring of the year.

IV.

What vows of affection we plighted,
   What dreams 'mid those high hills we wove,
Of glory and bliss, ever lighted
   And warmed by the gay lamp of love—
Those vows live by doubt still unhaunted,
   The gay lamp shines steady and clear,
Still brightening those dreams that enchanted
   In the soft blooming spring of the year.

V.

The future for us may be laden
   With grief, 'stead of bliss and of fame,
But I and my dear Irish maiden
   Shall love to the end still the same—
So sure to that love we'll be clinging,
   As flowers in our wild woods appear,
Or birds in green Ireland are singing
   In the soft blooming spring of the year.

THE OUTLAW OF KILMORE.

Air—" The wicked Kerryman".

I.

Far in the mountains with you, my Eveleen,
I would be loving and true, my Eveleen,
   Then climb the mountains with me.
Long have I dwelt by the forest river side,
Where the bright ripples flash and quiver wide,
There the fleet hours shall blissful ever glide
   O'er us, sweet Gra Gal Machree.

II.

There on my rocky throne, my Eveleen,
Ever, ever alone, my Eveleen,
   I sit dreaming of thee;
High on the fern-clad rocks reclining there,
Though the sweet birds their songs are twining fair,
Thee I hear—and I see thy shining hair
   Still, still, sweet Gra Gal Machree!

III.

Hunted and banned I've been, my Eveleen,
But my long sword is keen, my Eveleen,
   To keep all danger from thee:
The flash of this sword is my foeman's warning light,
And I live 'mid the wild hills scorning might,
While my love grows eve and morning bright
   For you, sweet Gra Gal Machree!

IV.

Deeply in broad Kilmore, my Eveleen,
Down by the wild stream's shore, my Eveleen,
   I've made a sweet home for thee;
Yellow and bright like thy long, long flowing hair,
Flowers the fairest are ever blowing there,—
Fairer still with thy clear eyes glowing there
   Fondly, sweet Gra Gal Machree!

V.

Then come away, away, my Eveleen;
We will spend each day, my Eveleen,
   Blissful and loving and free—
Come to the woods where the streams are pouring blue,
Which the eagle is ever soaring thro';
I'll grow fonder, each day adoring you,
   There, there, sweet Gra Gal Machree.

THE LOCKS OF AMBER.
Air—"Nora an cul omhra".

Her eyes beamed so clearly
   With love's sunny ray,
When I told her how dearly
   I loved her alway,

As she sat in the chamber
  'Mid gladness and light
With her long locks of amber
  All glossy and bright.

II.

There are shells by the sea-side
  Of brown golden hue,
There are flowers by the lea-side
  To mate with them, too:
The high rocks I clamber
  With gold-moss are dight—
Like my love's locks of amber
  All glossy and bright.

III.

When clouds gold and dun set
  O'er ocean and strand,
The deep hues of sunset
  Look glorious and grand:
Oh! they make me remember
  With endless delight
My love's locks of amber
  All glossy and bright.

IV.

One dear lock, I wear it,
  My fond maiden gave;
Nigh my heart I will bear it
  Till cold in my grave:—
Should life low'r like December,
  They'd give my heart light,
Those long locks of amber
  All glossy and bright!

ALLISDRUM'S MARCH AT THE BATTLE OF KNOCKINOSS.

A.D. 1648.

Air—"Allisdrum's March".

I.

Blow up the pipes with the brave battle chorus—
Look to your banner, the foe is before us—
Steady your guns, but when wanting to slay more,
There's nought like the rush and the slash of the claymore!
  Follow me, follow me, dauntless and steady,
  Shoulder to shoulder; the battle is ready;
  Many a foeman will ne'er see a day more,
  When we blow up the pipes and fall on with the claymore!

II.

Up Knockinoss comes he, Murrogh the Burner,*
The scourge of his race, of the Old Faith the spurner;
Black be the day he returned into Ireland,
To change her from peace to a woeful and dire land!
  Follow me, follow me, dauntless and steady,
  Shoulder to shoulder; the battle is ready:
  Look to your guns, but when wanting to slay more,
  Blow louder the pipes and fall on with the claymore!

---

* Murrogh O'Brien, Baron of Inchiquin, who fought at this time for Cromwell and the Parliamentarians.

III.

On down the hill, and ne'er fire till you're near them,
Then try from your path with one volley to clear them;
Down with your guns then, and up with your claymore,
And fast from our onset they'll soon clear the way more!
  Follow me, follow me, dauntless and steady,
  Shoulder to shoulder; the battle is ready;
  For God and our country we'll never delay more
  To blow up the pipes and fall on with the claymore!

IV.

Crash thro' the foe went that chief and his brave men,
With bosoms the stoutest that ever God gave men;
But curst be the day when Lord Taaffe grew faint-hearted,
And stood not, nor charged, but in panic departed!
  Leaving that chief with his comrades to die there,
  Leaving their corses for th' eagles to lie there;
  But the foeman he rued and remembered each day more
  Stout Allisdrum's march, and the sweep of his claymore!

THE LITTLE BIRD.

AIR—"As I was riding out one day".

A little bird with golden wings
  Flies past from bloom to blossom:
'Tis like the memory that springs
  Of you within my bosom;—

He flies unto the woodland tree,
    The tree he best loves only:
And thus that memory comes to me,
    Where'er I wander lonely.

II.

That little bird, some magic power,
    Some spell has surely found him,
For when he warbles in his bower,
    The woods seem glad around him;
And when I hear his dulcet voice,
    I think of yours each day, love,
And memory makes my heart rejoice,
    And I am glad and gay, love.

III.

I miss him now the woods among
    'Mid dewy leaves adorning:
The wild hawk heard his lonely song,
    And killed him in the morning;
But nought can kill the memory
    Of you, now sweetly shining
Within my heart so constantly,
    Till life that heart's resigning.

LAMENT OF GARODH EARLA.

A.D. 1582.

Air—"The night is coming".

I.

The night is coming, with black clouds looming,
    With thunders' booming, and wild winds' moan;
The fierce wolf's yelling from Corrin swelling,
    Our fate seems telling with mournful tone;

The dark cave's o'er us, deep floods before us
    With maddening chorus down rough rocks pour,
Yet love beams clearly, tho' we sit drearly,
    On death's brink nearly, by Mulla's shore.

II.

What dreams were mine, love, ere hope's decline, love,
    In war to shine, love, for Innisfail;
Aye to defend her from those that rend her,
    And cloud the splendour of the dauntless Gael;—
I reared each castle, I roused each vassal
    From sloth and wassail, to grasp the spear,
And aye thro' gory red fields of glory
    Bright triumph bore me for many a year.

III.

And oh! I quailed not while true hearts failed not,
    But blood availed not to set her free,
For those whose might, love, should still e'en smite, love,
    Grew faint in fight, love, and false to me;—
My power is broken, and each proud token
    Of Erin woken has died away;
For each endeavour will fail for ever,
    While brave hearts sever, and friends betray!

IV.

We've now for vassal and lordly castle
    And blithe friends' wassail, this cave of gloom,
With cold winds sighing round the embers dying;
    Yet still defying, we'll meet our doom,—
One joy will flourish, tho' power may perish,
    That joy we'll cherish—we'll love the more,
And love beams clearly, tho' we sit drearly,
    On death's brink nearly, by Mulla's shore!

MARY EARLEY.

Air—"The little fairy moat".

I.

There is an island on the lake
    Where dwelt my Mary Earley,
My modest maid with smile so sweet,
    And teeth so white and pearly,
With graceful form, and heart so warm,
    And eyes that shone so clearly,
And wild I loved, and wild adored,
    My sweet young Mary Early.

II.

There is a boat upon that lake,
    With sails of snowy whiteness,
That floats across the silent tide,
    From shore to shore in brightness,
And oft within that swan-like boat,
    While morn was shining fairly,
I've basked me in the sunny smiles
    Of loving Mary Earley.

III.

And oft upon the silent eves
    Of golden summer weather
We've sailed away to some bright bay,
    With joyful hearts together;
The wild birds seemed to haunt that shore,
    To sing around us rarely,
And many a song of love they sang
    For me and Mary Earley.

IV.

One autumn day to bar my way
    To love and that green island,
The storm swept down the moorlands brown,
    And roared o'er glen and highland;

I plunged me in the surging tide,
　And soon I clasped her dearly,
And kissed her by the island's side,
　My loving Mary Earley.

v.

And now beside Lough Deirgert's shore
　I sigh for Mary Earley,
And song birds all unheeded pour
　The strains they sing so rarely.
There is a ruin lone and hoar
　Where sigh the sad winds drearly,
And there she sleeps for evermore,
　My loving Mary Earley.

DIARMID MOR.

Air—" Says the mother to the daughter".

I.

The wintry sun with cheerless gleam
　Gilds Limerick's battered towers,
But far away down Shannon's stream
　A cloud of darkness lowers;
And there they glide upon the tide,
　The ships that bear him o'er
The stormy wave, with Sarsfield brave,
　My gallant Diarmid Mor.

II.

One summer eve long, long ago,
　He said by wandering Lee,
Its rushing waves should backward flow
　Ere he would part from me;

But war came down, with darkest frown,
   And called from Shannon shore—
He left his bride that eventide,
   My gallant Diarmid Mor.

III.

He heard its call, and sped away
   To aid his native land.
Can Aughrim's field, or Limerick say
   They saw a truer hand?
Heart, arm, and glaive he freely gave,
   As did his sires before—
And now he flees across the seas,
   My gallant Diarmid Mor.

IV.

By Lee's green banks the flowers shall bloom
   When summer decks the grove,
But when unto my heart shall come
   The smiles of my true love?
Oh! oft and drear shall flow the tear,
   Till some glad bark has bore
My love again back o'er the main,
   My gallant Diarmid Mor.

ALLEY KELLY O!

Air—"Up the foggy mountain".

I.

Up the foggy mountain,
   Within the airy valley O!
Beside the summer fountain
   I met my Alley Kelly O!
Her neck than wood-rose whiter,
   Her lips the glowing cherry O!
You'd find no maiden brighter,
   From Sliab-na-man to Kerry O!

II.

Her hair in streams of glory
    Fell curling down so grandly O!
When by that mountain hoary
    My love stood smiling blandly O!
I thought the Queen of Faery
    That highland valley haunted O!
When 'neath the green trees airy
    I sat me down enchanted O!

III.

My heart was flaming wildly,
    My voice with love was trembling O!
Her words came low and mildly,
    The harp's sweet tone resembling O!
I told her by the water,
    While sang the wild birds clearly O!
That up the hills I sought her,
    And that I loved her dearly O!

IV.

Within my heart I blessed her,
    She looked so fondly smiling O!
And to my bosom pressed her,
    Sweet kisses love beguiling O!
And still to that dear fountain
    Within the airy valley O!
I oft stray o'er the mountain
    To meet my Alley Kelly O!

MY FLOWER OF FLOWERS.
Air—" Slan Beo".

I.

Far, far away, where the valleys are fair and green,
And the Suir murmurs down its castles and wild
    woods between,
And the beautiful hills shine grand in the sunset
    hours,
With a heart full of sorrow I first met my flower
    of flowers.

II.

With grief in my heart—but sorrow is ne'er so sad
But fondness can lighten and true-love can make it
    glad;
And fondness and true love I found by the Suir's
    green bowers,
When I pledged her my troth and worshipped my
    flower of flowers.

III.

Oh! fair is the rose that smiles in Anner's green
    dale,
And modest and pure is the lily so pearly and pale,
And the eyebright shines like a star from Heaven's
    blue towers:
But fairer to me is my beautiful flower of flowers.

IV.

My heart's like a golden temple of fairyland
Since I first saw my love with her face so bright and
    bland,
And the world seems a path where never a dark
    cloud lowers—
For the sun that shines o'er is my beautiful flower
    of flowers.

THIS MAID OF MINE.

Air—"Costly were her robes of gold".

I.

My Mary is not wondrous fair
　　As other maidens are,
Yet she's to me a jewel rare,
　　A clear bright shining star;
No glorious form that can surprise,
　　No Grecian face divine—
The beauty of her soul-bright eyes
　　That marks this maid of mine.

II.

No vain pursuit, no idle thought,
　　No art its charm bestows;
No smiles with honeyed treachery fraught
　　My darling true-love knows;
A bashful mien, a modest face,
　　Where sunny health doth shine,
A form of sweet and simple grace
　　That mark this maid of mine.

III.

She dwells not in the lordly halls
　　Where fashion loves to blaze,
But where the rocks like giant walls
　　And hills their green sides raise;
And there no guile her heart has known,
　　No proud charms false and fine—
There trusting love for me alone
　　That marks this maid of mine.

FINEEN THE ROVER.

Air—" You'd think, if you heard their pipes squealing".

I.

An old castle towers o'er the billows
   That thunder by Cleena's green land,
And there dwelt as gallant a rover
   As ever grasped hilt in the hand;
Eight stately towers of the waters
   Lie anchored in Baltimore Bay,
And over their twenty score sailors,
   Oh! who but that Rover holds sway?
      Then ho! for Fineen the Rover,
         Fineen O'Driscoll the free,
      Straight as the mast of his galley,
         And wild as a wave of the sea!

II.

The Saxons of Cork and Moyallo,
   They harried his lands with their powers;
He gave them a taste of his cannon,
   And drove them like wolves from his towers;
The men of Clan London brought over
   Their strong fleet to make him a slave;
They met him by Mizan's wild highland,
   And the sharks crunched their bones 'neath the wave!
      Then ho! for Fineen the Rover,
         Fineen O'Driscoll the free,
      With step like the red stag of Beara,
         And voice like the bold sounding sea!

III.

Long time in that old battered castle,
   Or out on the waves with his clan,
He feasted, and ventured, and conquered,
   But ne'er struck his colours to man,—

In a fight 'gainst the foes of his country
   He died as a brave man should die,
And he sleeps 'neath the waters of Cleena
   Where the waves sing his *caoine* to the sky!
     Then ho! for Fineen the Rover,
       Fineen O'Driscoll the free,
     With eye like the osprey's at morning,
       And smile like the sun on the sea!

THE YELLOW HAIR.

AIR—"As I went forth one evening".

I.

You'd know my gentle true-love 'mid five hundred
   maidens fair,
By her smiles of pleasant sweetness and her wondrous golden hair,
By her step of airy lightness, like a fawn's in forest lone,
And her gushing, loving laughter, like a sweet flute's golden tone.
   Oh! the yellow, yellow hair! oh, the glittering yellow hair,
   Sweetly flowing, brightly glowing, o'er her neck and shoulders fair!

II.

With a violet-tinted ribbon, and a ribbon all of green,
Doth she bind those glossy tresses at the pleasant morning's sheen;

And all day they gleam and glitter, like a young
    queen's golden crown,
But she lets them flow at sunset in their yellow
    brightness down.
    Oh, the yellow, yellow hair! oh, the glittering
        yellow hair,
    Sweetly flowing, brightly glowing, o'er her neck
        and shoulders fair!

III.

Beyond the tall, great mountains, where sing the
    wild streams' tides,
Amid the airy greenwoods, my lovely maid resides;
And she'll give, when next I meet her, of that hair
    one ringlet band,
And I'll wear it in my bosom, ever wandering through
    the land.
    Oh, the yellow, yellow hair! oh, the glittering
        yellow hair,
    Sweetly flowing, brightly glowing, o'er her neck
        and shoulders fair!

OH! FAIR SHINES THE SUN ON GLENARA.

Air—"Glenara".

I.

Oh! fair shines the sun on Glenara,
And calm rest his beams on Glenara;
    But oh! there's a light
    Far dearer, more bright,
Illumines my soul in Glenara,
The light of thine eyes in Glenara.

II.

And sweet sings the stream of Glenara,
Glancing down through the woods like an arrow;
 But a sound far more sweet
 Glads my heart when we meet
In the green summer woods of Glenara,—
Thy voice by the wave of Glenara.

III.

And oh! ever thus in Glenara,
Till we sleep in our graves by Glenara,
 May thy voice sound as free
 And as kindly to me,
And thine eyes beam as fond in Glenara,
In the green summer woods of Glenara!

MY ANNA'S EYES.

Air—"The summer is come".

I.

Where shines the sun on Cummergh's dells,
Far, far away, my Anna dwells,
And there her eyes first beamed on me,
And chained my heart eternally.
 I sit alone, that memory rise
 Of sunny hopes and golden ties,
 Of smiles that beam like morning skies,
 Within her large, blue, loving eyes!

II.

Saint Anne's lone well is bordered round,
With golden moss and fairy mound;

There harebells glow like sapphire gem:
My Anna's eyes are blue like them.
  I sit alone, that memory rise
  Of sunny hopes and golden ties,
  Of smiles that beam like morning skies,
  Within my Anna's loving eyes!

III.

Where'er she walks by hill or stream,
On all those eyes of glory beam,
With sweet and gentle rays that are
Like splendours of the morning star.
  I sit alone that memory rise
  Of sunny hopes and golden ties,
  Of smiles that beam like morning skies,
  Within my Anna's loving eyes!

IV.

And there is more than common light,
Far dearer still, to make them bright,—
Fond rays, that pure and freshly dart
From sinless soul and sunny heart.
  Then lone I sit, that memory rise
  Of sunny hopes and golden ties,
  Of smiles that beam like morning skies,
  Within her large, blue, loving eyes!

THE BLIND GIRL OF GLENORE.

Air—"The summer shines around me".

I.

The summer shines around me,
  With its blooms and shady bowers,
But I cannot see the glory
  Of the meadows and the flowers;

Once to me the golden summer
  Was all one lapse of light,
Till the red, red lightning struck me,
  And withered up my sight.
    Ah! Donall, Donall,
      Donall of Glenore,
    Give me back the heart I gave you
      In the sunny days of yore.

II.

Do you mind the sunlit meadow
  Where the Funcheon murmurs past,
Where you vowed one silent even
  That your love should ever last?
I have now no friends to love me:
  In Molagga's yard lie they:
And the blindness, oh! the blindness
  Is upon me night and day!
    Ah! Donall, Donall,
      Donall of Glenore,
    Give me back the heart I gave you
      In the sunny days of yore.

III.

They tell me in the village
  That your heart to me is changed;
But your words have never told me
  That you wish to be estranged;
Yet I will not cloud the gladness
  Of a heart so kind and free—
Oh! this blindness, oh! this blindness,
  Sad the doom it brought to me!
    Ah! Donall, Donall,
      Donall of Glenore,
    Give me back the heart I gave you
      In the sunny days of yore.

IV.

Place your hand upon my temples,
   Feel the hot blood pulsing through;—
Is it pain of bitter sickness,
   Or pain of love for you?
'Tis the bitter, bitter fever
   That is burning in my brain,
While I strive that love to banish
   Till my heart-strings crack and strain.
     Ah! Donall, Donall,
       Donall of Glenore,
     Give me back the heart I gave you
       In the sunny days of yore.

V.

Donall took the hand of Nora
   On that lovely morning-tide,
He led her to the chapel,
   And he made her there his bride.
Oh! to find a pair so happy
   You should travel far and wide,
As the blind maid and her Donall
   By the Funcheon's flowery side!
     Ah! Donall, Donall,
       Donall of Glonore;
     Still he loved her, as he loved her
       In the sunny days of yore!

FAIR KATE OF GLENANNER.
Air—"Fair Kate".

I.

The sunlight is sleeping on Cummerah's wild mountain,
And gay shine the blossoms by dingle and fountain;
Sweet murmurs the stream where the soft breezes fan her,
And bright at my side sits fair Kate of Glenanner.

II.

The boughs of the elms in the cool breeze are
    swaying,
With the clear waves beneath toward the wide ocean
    playing,
And the tall ferns wave like a green sunlit banner,
While I whisper my love to fair Kate of Glenanner.

III.

She smiles as she points at the sunny wave near me,
And I wish for a boat with its white sail to bear me
From that spot, from the stream where the gray
    arches span her,
To some green isle of love with fair Kate of Glen-
    anner.

SONG OF THE FOREST FAIRY.

Air—"The Fairy Man".

I.

Where the golden moss hangs on the mighty oak,
Where never was heard the woodman's stroke,
  In the ancient woods
    Where the wild deer bide—
  Where the heron broods,
    By the lakelet's side,
Morn, noon, and eve, in the rosy air,
We dance full merrily there, oh, there!

I.

At night in a glade of the brightest green
We meet with fond homage our youthful queen:
  There in revel and feast
    We spend the night,
  Or in balmy rest
    Till the morning light,

When out on the greensward smooth and fair
We dance so merrily there, oh, there!

III.

'Tis glorious to see the globes of dew
By the red beams of morn pierced through and
    through;
  'Tis sweet to peer
    Where the wild-flower gleams,
  And sweeter to hear
    The birds and the streams;
And sweeter than all in the blue, bright air,
To dance so merrily there, oh, there!

MERRILY, MERRILY PLAYING.

AIR—"Gleantaun Araglin ĕving".

I.

Merrily, merrily playing,
  Dances the rill away,
Where breezes soft are straying
  And linnets sing all day;
Sweeter than wood-rill's glee is,
  Sweeter than linnet's tune,
My Helen's voice to me is,
  All in the rose-bright June.

II.

I sit by Corrin's highland,
  Her dear hand clasped in mine,
While wood and stream-girt island
  Glow in the noon-day shine;
The stream is sweetly welling,
  The flowers are round us strewn,
And we our love are telling
  All in the rose-bright June.

III.

My love than the rose is sweeter
  That blooms in yonder dell,
And far I've come to meet her,
  For oh! she loves me well;
And the stream by the gay beams lighted
  Shall freeze in the summer noon,
Ere we break the vows we've plighted
  All in the rose-bright June.

THE SIEGE OF LIMERICK.

Air—"Cūl awling deas".

I.

By William led, the English sped,
  With musket, sword, and cannon,
To sweep us all from Limerick's wall,
  And drown us in the Shannon;
But we bethought how well they fought,
  Our fathers there before us;
We raised on high our charging cry,
  And flung our green flag o'er us!

II.

For days on days their cannon's blaze
  Flashed by the blood-stained water;—
The breach is done, and up they run,
  Five hundred to the slaughter;
They crossed the breach beyond our reach—
  New foes fresh work supplied us—
Our women brave, their homes to save,
  Soon slew them all inside us!

III.

Though through the smoke their army broke,
    With cannons booming solemn,
We would not flinch, but inch for inch
    Opposed each bristling column;
Three times we dashed them back, and smashed
    Their lines with shot and sabre,
And nought had they at close of day
    But thinned ranks for their labour.

IV.

With angry word then said their lord,
    "Our foes are better, braver!"
Then fled he straight from Limerick's gate,
    For he could not enslave her;
Then raised we high our triumph cry,
    Where battle's chances found us,
With corse, and gun, and rent flags strewn,
    And blood and ruin round us!

FAIR HELEN OF THE DELL.

Air—"The Dark Maid of the Dell".

I.

Though joy his flow'rs be twining,
And thou in beauty shining,
Yet oh! in joy's declining
    I'd love thee still as well;
Wherever fortune lead thee,
Or wind or wave can speed thee,
This true heart still shall heed thee,
    Fair Helen of the Dell.

II.

I've never yet beholden
A form so finely moulden,
Thy hair a sunset golden,
   Thy voice the clear harp's swell;
Thine eyes have Heav'n's own brightness,
Thy neck the lily's whiteness,
Thy step the hill-stream's lightness,
   Fair Helen of the Dell.

III.

Few summers thou hast numbered;
Thy heart to this has slumbered;
Love leads it now uncumbered
   In his bright bowers to dwell;
He casts his splendour o'er thee,
He walks in light before thee,
That I may wild adore thee,
   Fair Helen of the Dell.

THE DRINAN DHUN.

Air—"The Drinan Dhun".

I.

By road and by river the wild birds sing;
O'er mountain and valley the dewy leaves spring;
The gay flowers are shining, gilt o'er by the sun;
And fairest of all shines the Drinán Dhun.

II.

The rath of the fairy, the ruin hoar,
With white silver splendour it decks them all o'er;
And down in the valleys where merry streams run,
How sweet smell the blossoms of the Drinán Dhun.

III.

Ah! well I remember the soft spring day
I sat by my love 'neath its sweet-scented spray;
The day that she told me her heart I had won,
Beneath the white blossoms of the Drinán Dhun.

IV.

The streams they were singing their gladsome song,
The soft winds were blowing the wildwoods among,
The mountains shone bright in the red setting sun,
And my love in my arms 'neath the Drinán Dhun!

V.

'Tis my prayer in the morning, my dream at night,
To sit thus again by my heart's dear delight,
With her blue eyes of gladness, her hair like the sun,
And her sweet, loving kisses, 'neath the Drinán Dhun.

WHATEVER WIND IS BLOWING.

Air—" Where have you been?"

I.

My heart's not made to freeze and fade
  On sorrow's stony mountains,
But aye it turns, and oh! it burns
  To drink at pleasure's fountains!
    Then I will drink what best I think
      To cool its hot thirst glowing,
    And love shall be first guide to me,
      Whatever wind is blowing.

II.

When woe calls down night's darksome frown,
  With not a star for warning,
One thought of two sweet eyes of blue
  Soon brings the glorious morning.
    Still o'er my way with blessed ray
      May love's calm light be glowing,
    And honour too still guide me through,
      Whatever wind is blowing.

MARYANNE.

AIR—"John the journeyman".

I.

In sweet Tipperary dwells my love,
Where Sliabhnamon stands tall above,
And from that hill to banks of Ban
There's not a girl like Maryanne.
  Oh! fair the face of Maryanne!
  Oh! warm the heart of Maryanne!
  From Sliabhnamon to northern Ban
  There's not a girl like Maryanne.

II.

My girl is artless as a child,
So fair and modest, fond and mild;
Not all the verses made by man
Could tell the charms of Maryanne.
  Oh! fair the face of Maryanne!
  Oh! fond the heart of Maryanne!
  Not all the verses made by man
  Could tell the charms of Maryanne.

III.

Her glossy hair is black as night,
And dark, deep blue her eyes of light—
Like midnight stars o'er Heaven's blue span,
The sparkling eyes of Maryanne.

Oh! fair the face of Maryanne!
Oh! fond the heart of Maryanne!
Like midnight stars o'er Heaven's blue span,
The sparkling eyes of Maryanne.

IV.

My soul is sad, my heart is sore,
To think I ne'er may see her more;
For ne'er was girl, since youth began,
So dear to me as Maryanne!
   Oh! fair the face of Maryanne!
   Oh! warm the heart of Maryanne!
   From Sliabhnamon to northern Ban
   There's not a girl like Maryanne!

MY FIRST LOVE.

Air—"My love is like a summer day".

I.

Where towers the rock above the trees,
   With heath-bells blooming o'er;
Where waves the fern in summer breeze,
   And shines the red lusmore;
In woodland nook beside the brook,
   I sit and sadly pore
On love I nursed in boyhood first
   For one I'll ne'er see more.

II.

How fair, when shines the summer beam
   Upon the mountains warm,
The lady fern beside the stream—
   As fair my Margaret's form:
The snow-white crystals shine beneath,
   The red lusmores above,—
Ah! such the bright, bright laughing teeth
   And lips of my first love!

III.

The gorse flowers Ullair's dells illume,
  One sea of golden light;
My Margaret's hair was like their bloom,
  As yellow and as bright:
'Twill haunt me still, thro' joy or ill,
  Till death shall end my care,—
The wondrous grace of her fair face
  Beneath that golden hair.

VI.

I loved her with a burning love
  That matched my boyhood well,
And brilliant were the dreams I wove
  While tranced in that sweet spell;
And in my breast she'll reign and rest
  Each eve while sad I pore,
Where ferns are green the banks between,
  And shines the red lusmore!

I SIT ON THE HOLD OF MOYALLO.

Air—"Thro' Mallow without my armour".

I.

I sit on the hold of Moyallo,
  And look on the Blackwater stream,
As it bounds from the moors of Duhallow,
  And shines in the gay summer beam:
And I dream of a nation uprisen
  From its dark night of bondage and gloom—
A captive, long pining in prison,
  Restored to day's beauty and bloom.

II.

I look from the light dancing water,
   O'er steep hill, and wild wood, and mound,
Where many a dark day of slaughter
   Hath reddened the green vales around:
Of vengeance I am not a dreamer
   For the true blood there spilt long ago,
Tho' I dream that mere words won't redeem her,
   Green Erin, from bondage and woe.

III.

Long, long we have asked to restore us
   Our freedom, and still we are slaves:
'Twas thus with our fathers before us,
   And bondsmen they went to their graves:
The wish, and the faint heart to slack it,
   Have failed, since the green earth began;
The wish, and the brave hand to back it,
   'Tis that makes the patriot man!

IV.

From the north to the blue south'rn water,
   Who wish for their freedom again,
Should ask no revenge for each slaughter,
   But rise up like brave, honest men;
And when by the word or the sabre
   We've righted the wrongs we deplore,
Like men, and not slaves, with our neighbour
   We'd prosper in peace evermore.

THE RAPPAREE'S HORSE AND SWORD.

Air.—" Oh! say, my brown drimin".

I.

My name is Mac Sheehy, from Feal's swelling flood,
A rapparee rover by mountain and wood:
I've too trusty comrades to serve me at need,—
This sword at my side and my gallant gray steed.

Now where did I get them,—my gallant gray steed,
And this sword keen and trusty to serve me at need?
This sword was my father's—in battle he died—
And I reared bold Isgur by Feal's woody side.

III.

I've said it, and say it, and care not who hear,
Myself and gray Isgur have never known fear:
There's a dint on my helmet, a hole thro' his ear:
'Twas the same bullet made them at Lim'rick last year!

IV.

And the soldier who fired it was still ramming down,
When this long sword came right with a slash on his crown;
Dhar Dhia! but he'll ne'er fire a musket again,
For his skull lies in two at the side of the glen!

V.

When they caught us one day at the castle of Brugh,
Of our black-hearted foemen the deadliest crew,
Like a bolt from the thunder gray Isgur went through,
And my sword! long they'll weep at the sore taste of you!

VI.

Together we sleep 'neath the wild crag or tree,—
My soul! but there ne'er were such comrades as we!
I, Brian the Rover, my two friends at need,
This sword at my side and my gallant gray steed!

MY MARY.
AIR—"My Mary".

I.

My Mary's far from me
  By the banks of wild Blackwater,
Where she sings full mournfully
  The old love songs I taught her—
Ever sings that sweetest tune,
"*Shule aroon*", soft "*shule aroon,*
Come to me, and come full soon",
  By the banks of wild Blackwater.

II.

My Mary's blue eyes speak
  The love that lights her bosom;
My Mary's lips and cheek
  Are like the red rose blossom;
Through miles of frost and sleet
I'd go, with naked feet,
To kiss those lips so sweet,
  And clasp her to my bosom.

III.

Through north and south countrie
  I've seen full many a maiden,
And fair they were and free,
  With many a sweet charm laden;—

Their charms were fair to view,
But oh! for fondness true,
I'll ne'er meet one like you,
    My own young Munster maiden.

IV.

The rocks may wear to sand,
    By the banks of wild Blackwater,
But firm my love shall stand
    For Armoy's fairest daughter,
As she sings that old sweet tune—
"*Shule aroon*", soft "*shule aroon,*
Come to me, and come full soon",
    By the banks of wild Blackwater.

SONG OF TREN THE FAIRY.

AIR—"The fairy companie".

I.

From flower bells of each hue,
    Crystal-white, or golden yellow,
Purple, violet, red, or blue,
We drink the honey-dew
    Until we all get mellow—
    Until we all get mellow,
    And thro' our festal glee,
I'm the blithest little fellow
    In the fairy companie.

II.

In the fairy companie
    They call me Trén the Merry,
And no name's so fit for me,
For I love in revelry
    Each gloomy thought to bury—
    Each dark, sad thought to bury,

As I laugh by flower and tree,
  Hill, stream, and river ferry,
    Midst the fairy companie.

III.

'Neath the sunset's purple ray
  Cups of purple wine we swallow;
Then I laugh, and sing, and play,
And my fairy mates are gay,
  And where'er I go they follow;
  With laughter mad they follow,
    I dance so merrilie,
  O'er hill and flowered-star'd hollow,
    For the fairy companie.

IV.

Our brightest, favourite spot
  Is in a Munster wildwood,
Where the foot of man comes not,
And the rays are ne'er too hot,
  And the stream-voice clear and mild would—
  Merry, low, and sweet, and mild—would
    Make the dead leap up in glee,
  And the flowers keep in their childhood
    For the fairy companie.

V.

There from bells of many a hue,
  Crystal white, or golden yellow,
The blissful summer through,
We drink the honey dew,
  Until we all get mellow—
  Laughing, quaffing, glad, and mellow,
    And thro' our festal glee,
  I'm the blithest little fellow
    In the fairy companie!

BRAVE DONALL.

Air—"Donal's Lament".

I.

I stray alone by cove and cave,
With sad eyes looking o'er the wave,
And heart as mournful as the grave,
Since I lost my lover brave!
    Oh! my brave Donall!
    My bold, brave Donall!
My heart is in your foreign grave,
    My bold, brave Donall!

II.

Not all unknown his soldier sire;
Like glory did my love require;
Till fame grew in his heart of fire
A burning and a wild desire!
    Oh! my brave Donall!
    My bold, brave Donall!
What more than love could you require,
    My bold, brave Donall?

III.

Away to France my true love sped,
To join the bold Brigade, he said;
'Twas 'neath its flag in battle red
His only brother fought and bled!
    Oh! my brave Donall!
    My bold, brave Donall!
With fair, false hopes my heart you fed,
    My bold, brave Donall!

IV.

'Twas mounting on the foeman's wall
My gallant true love met his fall,
But dying, saw his banner tall
Waving in victory over all!
    Oh! my brave Donall!
    My bold, brave Donall!
For me they weave the funeral pall,
    My bold, brave Donall!

V.

And thus I stray where Shannon's wave
Moans mournfully by cove and cave,
My sad heart in that far-off grave,
Where sleeps in gore my lover brave!
    Oh! my brave Donall!
    My bold, brave Donall!
My heart is withering in your grave,
    My bold, brave Donall!

I STILL AM A ROVER.

Air—"Bundle and go".

I.

I still am a rover our green island over,
  A passion-fraught lover of beauty and bloom,
On wild mountains pondering, thro' sweet valleys
    wandering,
  Where soft winds are squandering the blossom's
    perfume;

From all those dear places the bland summer graces,—
From all their fair faces my heart still doth stray,
Where clear waves are flinging, and flowerets are springing,
And blithe birds are singing in sunny Gleneigh!

II.

There green woods wave slowly to winds breathing lowly,
And ruin walls holy stand gray o'er the scene;
There clear fountains rally their strength in each valley,
Where waves the wild sally and birch leaves are green;
There rocks famed in story stand silent and hoary,
And fields in the glory of summer are gay,
And mead blossoms muster their bells of bright lustre,
And rich berries cluster in sunny Gleneigh!

III.

Yet 'tis not the tender sweet beauty and splendour
That dwells there can render such joy to my breast;
'Tis love has arrayed it, and decked and displayed it,
As spring never made it, or mild summer dress'd:
There Gracie is dwelling in beauty excelling,
Her bright looks still telling love ne'er can decay,
While clear waves are flinging, and flowerets are springing,
And blithe birds are singing in sunny Gleneigh.

THERE IS A TREE IN DARRA'S WOOD.
Air—"Barrack Hill".

I.

There is a tree in Darra's wood
    That bears the rose-red berry,
Where sweetly sings the fairy flood
    With cadence wild and merry;—
O love! like berries of that tree,
    Thy red lips smile so dearly,
And like that stream's glad minstrelsy
    Thy laugh rings soft and clearly!
        So clearly, so clearly,
           So witching, soft, and clearly,
        That evermore I must adore
           And love thee, true love, dearly!

II.

Beneath that tree I've built a bower,
    Its roof with love-knots twining,
And there the snowy shamrock flower
    And blue-bells gay are shining,—
I've built a bower within my breast
    And placed thee on its throne, love,
And ever there I'll love thee best,
    My dark-eyed Grace, my own love!
        My own love, my own love,
           I've have placed thee on its throne, love,
        And day and night, for ever bright,
           There you shall reign, my own love!

III.

'Mid Darra's wood a castle tall
    Stands wrecked with age, and hoary;
A white rose tree hangs from its wall
    With blooms of star-like glory;—

Thy fair brow hath that rose's hue,
  Kind nature's own adorning:
Thy heart is stainless as the dew
    That gems its leaves at morning:—
      At morning, at morning,
        When dew that flower's adorning,
      When out I rove thro' Darra's grove,
        To think on thee at morning.

IV.

Oh! still may wane the summer moon,
  The gay flowers follow after;
The merry birds may hush their tune,
  And glad streams cease their laughter;
The leaves may wither on the tree,
  All things grow cold and drear, love,
But that sweet bower I've built to thee
  Shall ever bloom, my dear love!
    My dear love, my dear love,
      You'll reign without a peer, love,
      That bower within, the glorious queen
      Of my fond heart, my dear love!

I BUILT ME A BOWER.
Air—"Gouan gal bān".

I.

I built me a bower in life's greenwood,
  A palace of blooms for my soul,
And there on the maids all unseen would
  I dream 'neath love's blissful control,
Till I set up the image of Alice
  Supreme on my heart's burning throne;
Then long in my flow'r-woven palace
  I bowed to that image alone.

II.

Oh! fair was my bird of the mountains,
   Oh! sweet as the thorn's scented spray,
Oh! pure as the light of the fountains
   That dance down the green hills in May.
A chapter of joy-woven story,
   A voyage o'er a bright fairy sea,
A May-tide of bloom and of glory
   Were the days of our love-time to me.

III.

But the chapter oft ends all in sorrow,
   The voyage hath its tempests and gloom,
And the May-tide, though bright be each morrow,
   Must pass, like our lives, to the tomb;—
Oh! the dreams of my love-time are humbled,
   The blooms from my green bow'r are fled,
My idol lies shattered and crumbled,
   My Alice, my sweet flow'r, is dead!

FAIR MAIDENS' BEAUTY WILL SOON FADE AWAY.

Air—"My love she was born in the north countrie".

I.

My love she was born in the south countrie,
Where Cork's sunny highlands look over the Lee;
My love is as fair as the soft smiling May;
But fair maidens' beauty will soon fade away.

II.

My love is as pure as the bright blessed well
That springs all so lonely in Gartan's green dell;
My love she is graceful, and tender, and gay;
But fair maidens' beauty will soon fade away.

III.

My love is as sweet as the cinnamon tree;
As the bark to its bough cleaves she firm unto me;
Its green leaves will wither and its roots will decay,
So fair maidens' beauty will soon fade away.

IV.

But love, though the green leaf may wither and fall,
Though the bright eye be dimmed, and the sweet smile and all,—
Oh! love has a life that may never decay,
Though fair maidens' beauty will soon fade away.

V.

And the true-hearted maid of the south countrie,
Should the bright angels bear her to Heaven from me,
There she'd love me as fond as she loves me to-day,
Though fair maidens' beauty will soon fade away.

THE CAILIN RUE.

Air—"An Cailin Ruadh".

I.

When first I sought her by Cashin's water,
   Fond love I brought her, fond love I told;
At day's declining I found her twining
   Her bright locks shining like red, red gold.
She raised her eyes then in sweet surprise then—
   Ah! how unwise then such eyes to view!
For free they found me, but fast they bound me,
   Love's chain around me for my Cailin Rue.

II.

Fair flowers were blooming, the meads illuming,
   All fast assuming rich summer's pride,
And we were roving, truth's rapture proving,
   Ah! fondly loving, by Cashin's side;

Oh! love may wander, but ne'er could sunder
  Our hearts, that fonder each moment grew,
Till friends delighted such love requited,
  And my hand was plighted to my Cailin Rue.

III.

Ere May's bright weather o'er hill and heather,
  Sweet tuned together rang our bridal bells:
But at May's dying, on fate relying,
  Fate left us sighing by Cashin's dells;
Oh! sadly perished the bliss we cherished!
  But far lands flourished o'er the ocean blue,
So as June came burning I left Erin mourning,
  No more returning with my Cailin Rue.

IV.

Our ship went sailing with course unfailing,
  But black clouds trailing lowered o'er the main,
And its wild dirge singing, came the storm out springing,
  That good ship flinging back, back again!
A sharp rock under tore her planks asunder,
  While the sea in thunder swallowed wreck and crew;
One dark wave bore me where the coast towered o'er me,
  But dead before me lay my Cailin Rue!

THE GREEN RIBBON.

Air—"The green ribbon".

I.

I met my love in the woodland screen
  With fond and sweet caresses;
I gave my love a ribbon green
  To bind her yellow tresses;

She loosed each long lock's shining fold
　　O'er her neck of snowy whiteness,
And she bound the green with the yellow gold
　　In braids of glossy brightness.

II.

It was beside a murmuring rill
　　Which through the woods descended,
And over peaceful vale and hill
　　The sun shone calm and splendid;
Oh! often 'mid those leafy bowers
　　In sweet blooms I arrayed her;
But lovelier far than summer flowers
　　That bright green ribbon made her.

III.

Then oh! she minded how the green
　　Was oft' triumphant waving,
When long ago beneath its sheen
　　Our sires the foe were braving—
I'd brave red death on sea or land
　　To change our country's story,
And gladly die at my love's command
　　To give the green new glory!

IV.

But ne'er was heart of maiden yet
　　Than hers more true or fonder,
And aye she pines in sad regret
　　While far away I wander;
Oh! still through every changing scene
　　Our fond love shall be glowing,
While the leaves shine as that ribbon green,
　　And the wild rill's tide is flowing.

ANNIE DE CLARE.

Air—"The merry dancers".

I.

The rill at its fountain how calm is its flowing!
The rill down the mountain comes rushing and
    glowing—
True love in my breast like its tide's ever growing,
  Since I saw the bright eyes of my Annie de Clare.

II.

Oh! blest be the hours that I last saw them beaming
In her home of the Crag, by the waterfall's stream-
    ing—
How I scaled the wild rocks with the red sunset
    gleaming,
  Up into the arms of my Annie de Clare!

III.

Oh! the glory that lay o'er the green earth and
    heaven!
Oh! the sweet lapse of bliss to my fond bosom given,
As I sat by the stream on that calm summer even
  In the love-lighted smiles of my Annie de Clare.

IV.

Many and bright were the pleasures that crowned me,
And dear the enchantments since boyhood that bound
    me,
But dearer than all were the fond arms round me,
  And the red rosy lips of my Annie de Clare.

V.

When the ardour of love lights the soul with its
    splendour,
No cares may annoy her, no sorrows can rend her;
So my soul's wrapt in gladness with visions all tender
  Of glory and love and my Annie de Clare.

VI.

And glory may crown me, of bright meeds the giver,
But love hath a guerdon more blissful for ever,
That bower where we sat by the wild Mumhan river
   And the fond, twining arms of my Annie de Clare.

THE MARCH OUT OF LIMERICK.

Air—" The Rapparee's March".

I.

Comrades true, to dare and do,
   Oh! they are few who've yet denied us;
We'll not say they could betray,
   For many a day they fought beside us;
By hill and glade, in fight and raid,
   With vengeful blade we smote the foeman,
And now till we find Ireland free
   Our banner-tree shall droop to no man.

II.

Alas, for strife! child, parent, wife,
   More dear than life, we leave behind us;
They weep full sore, but on this shore
   Oh! never more in joy they'll find us:—
More blest the brave in bloody grave,
   By Boyne's red wave, or Aughrim sleeping,
Than we who hear our children dear,
   And fond friends near thus wildly weeping!

III.

Sarsfield stands before our bands,
   For foreign lands his words prepare us;
By Thomond Gate the Dutchmen wait,
   Their flag elate, but to ensnare us;

In serried mass our bright files pass
    With steel cuirass and helmet gleaming,
Our brave choice said by onward tread,
    And green flag spread above us streaming.

IV.

Yon mournful train they weep in vain,
    Black woe and pain their steps attending;—
And think of all who met their fall
    Brave Limerick's wall so long defending;
When we look back on war's grim wrack,
    On turret black and breach all gory,
By hearthstone bare and breach we swear,
    Revenge to share, come grief or glory!

V.

Farewell ye Dead, who nobly bled;
    Your blood was shed for Ireland's honour,
To change her doom, to chase the gloom
    Whose shadows loom so dark upon her;
And ye farewell, whose wild cries swell,
    A mournful knell, at home to bind us,
Your hearts full sore on th' Irish shore
    For evermore we leave behind us!

FAINGE AN LAE.*

AIR—"Fainge an lae".

I.

The sun in his splendour and glory
    Sets over the shining main,
And island and precipice hoary
    Are swimming in gold again;

---

* *Fainge an lae*—the dawning of the morning.

Ah! many a battle-field gory
　　He lights by that ocean's spray,
The scenes of each tragical story
　　Which darkened our Fainge an lae!

II.

The hill-tops of Clare are defining
　　Their shapes in the golden glow;
The mountains of Kerry are shining
　　Sublime on the plains below;
They look on a master still twining
　　The gyves of our woe each day;
They look on a race ever pining,
　　And all for our Fainge an lae.

III.

They mind me, so riven and valleyed,
　　Of bownocht* and rapparee,
Who oft' round their hoar summits rallied
　　To set their green country free.
Oh! these were the men that ne'er dallied
　　When once set in war's array,
But fierce on the scared foeman sallied,
　　And all for their Fainge an lae.

IV.

Fair Freedom soon, soon must awaken
　　With her form of sun-bright mould;
Then let her not wander forsaken,
　　But armed, as in days of old,—
With her green flags and banners outshaken
　　Oh! what could our triumph stay?
Our thirst for the right would be slaken—
　　We'd soon have our Fainge an lae!

---

* *Bownocht*—a foot soldier.

V.

When the power of the tyrant is riven,
    And swordless his blood-stained hand,
When the black clouds from Erin are driven,
    Oh! where is the brighter land?
And when shall that grand hour be given
    That sets us on Freedom's way?
When, like the great Dead, we have striven,
    And all for our Fainge an lae!

GRA GAL BAN.

Air—"A rifleman for me".

I.

There's an airy, graceful lightness in her form of beauteous mould,
And her face shines out divinely 'neath her locks of silken gold;
    There are lovely maidens dwelling
        Through the land from sea to sea,
    But in beauty bright excelling,
        Oh! my Gra Gal Bān for me!

II.

But dim is beauty's brightness unless the soul shine through
The smile upon the coral lip—the dark eye, or the blue.
    There are lovely maidens dwelling
        Through the land from sea to sea,
    But in soul-bright eyes excelling,
        Oh! my Gra Gal Bān for me!

III.

And though age may steal upon her, and her beauty
   all may fade,
Joy shall linger in the glances of my guileless mountain maid.
      There are lovely maidens dwelling
         Through the land from sea to sea,
      But in every grace excelling,
         Oh! my Gra Gal Bān for me!

IV.

For what makes age as gladsome as the golden day
   of youth?
'Tis the heart's unchanged affection and the soul's
   immortal truth.
      There are lovely maidens dwelling
         Through the land from sea to sea,
      But in truthful love excelling,
         Oh! my Gra Gal Bān for me!

DONALL NA GREINE.*

Air—"Domnall na Greine".

I.

Where rolls the tide of the wandering Mulla,
   Brilliantly gleaming, gushing and gleaming,
Young Donall lay in a sunny hollow,
   Lazily dreaming, thinking and dreaming;
And thus he lay all that sweet summer idle,
   Fleeing from labour, fleeing from labour,
When his left hand should hold the skian or the
      bridle,
   And his right the steel sabre, the keen cutting
      sabre;

---

* Donall of the sunshine.

And hurra! for ease and for love's bright
    story,
  Sang Donall na Greine! tall Donall na
    Greine!
For both he dreamed of, not war and glory,
  Donall na Greine! tall Donall na Greine!

II.

There built he many an airy castle,
  Towering and gleaming, towering and gleaming,
And peopled their halls with fair maid and vassal,
  In his wild dreaming, in his wild dreaming;
And ne'er one cause could he still discover,
  Why his ease should be broken, his sweet ease
    broken,
Till his love proved false, and his dreams were over,
  And he a rover—to sorrow awoken!
    Then hurra! hurra! for a life of labour,
      Sang Donall na Greine! tall Donall na
        Greine!
    The steed, the corselet, and flashing sabre,
      For Donall na Greine! bold Donall na
        Greine!

III.

His steed's black mane to the winds is streaming,
  By valley and highland, by moorland and high-
    land;
You'd stray from Bengore with the white spray
    gleaming,
  To Cleir's stormy island, to Oeir's stormy island,
Ere a better or doughtier man could meet you,
  Than Donall na Greine! tall Donall na Greine!
Or a fiercer, haughtier smile could greet you—
  Tall Donall na Greine! bold Donall na Greine!

And hurra! hurra! for a life of labour,
   Sang Donall na Greine! bold Donall na Greine!
The rushing charge and the flashing sabre
   For Donall na Greine! bold Donall na Greine!

IV.

Soon the rapparees all his brave brothers were sworn
   Through hardship and danger, through hardship and danger;
O'Hogan to battle was never borne
   So fleet on the stranger, the false hearted stranger—
Oh! to see him down on the foeman dashing,
   How fearless he bore him, how reckless he bore him!
With his sabre keen in his strong hand flashing,
   Through the Sassenaghs crashing—his green flag o'er him!
   And hurra! hurra! for a life of labour,
      Sang Donall na Greine! bold Donall na Greine!
   The rushing charge and the shining sabre,
      For Donall na Greine! bold Donall na Greine!

V.

Once again he loved, by the Shannon water,
   A maiden unchanging, with fond heart unchanging,
And after many a field of slaughter,
   Away they went ranging, to foreign lands ranging;—
At Fontenoy his brave generals paid him,
   Tall Donall na Greine! bold Donall na Greine!

A captain fine on that field they made him,
    For fear never swayed him, bold Donall na
        Greine!
      Then hurra! for love and a life of labour,
        Sang Donall na Greine! bold Donall na
          Greine!
      Unchanging love and a conquering sabre,
        For Donall na Greine! bold Donall na
          Greine!

THE COMING BRIDAL.

Air—" B'fearr liomsa ainnir gan gúna".

I.

My home stands by Funcheon's bright river,
    Where the broom blossoms shine in the spring,
Where the green beeches murmur and quiver,
    And the birds 'mid their cool branches sing;
And there where the sky gleams so blue in
    The stream as it winds through the dells,
A-down by the old castle ruin,
    My love in her white cottage dwells.

II.

The black whortle shines 'mid the heather,
    Where the wild deer in brown autumn rove,
And dark is the strong raven's feather,
    But darker the locks of my love;
Two trees by the Fort of the Fairy,
    A red rose and white, sweetly grow;
Oh! the lips and the brow of my Mary
    Outshine their pure crimson and snow.

III.

No flocks hath she down by the island,
  No red gold her coffers illume,
No herds over brown moor or highland,
  No meads where the sweet flow'rs may bloom;
The old dame hath herds by the wildwood,
  She'd give me herds, green meads, and gold,
But the young heart that loved me since childhood
  Shall find me in manhood unsold.

IV.

Next Sunday the fires will be blazing
  For the Baal-feast o'er mountain and plain;
That morn village crowds will be gazing
  With joy on our gay bridal train;—
Could love half so blest ever falter,
  When placed 'mid the throng side by side,
When there at the old chapel altar
  The good priest will make her my bride?

THE WIND THAT SHAKES THE BARLEY.

Air—"The old love and the new love".

I.

I sat within the valley green,
  I sat me with my true love,
My sad heart strove the two between,
  The old love and the new love,—
The old for her, the new that made
  Me think on Ireland dearly,
While soft the wind blew down the glade
  And shook the golden barley.

II.

'Twas hard the woeful words to frame
    To break the ties that bound us,—
'Twas harder still to bear the shame
    Of foreign chains around us;
And so I said, "The mountain glen
    I'll seek next morning early,
And join the brave United men!"
    While soft winds shook the barley.

III.

While sad I kissed away her tears,
    My fond arms round her flinging,
The foeman's shot burst on our ears,
    From out the wildwood ringing,—
The bullet pierced my true love's side,
    In life's young spring so early,
And on my breast in blood she died
    While soft winds shook the barley!

IV.

I bore her to the wildwood screen,
    And many a summer blossom
I placed with branches thick and green
    Above her gore-stain'd bosom:—
I wept and kissed her pale, pale cheek,
    Then rushed o'er vale and far lea,
My vengeance on the foe to wreak,
    While soft winds shook the barley!

V.

And blood for blood without remorse
    I've ta'en at Oulart Hollow,*—
I've placed my true-love's clay-cold corse
    Where I full soon will follow;

---

* The deep quarry on Oulart hill.

And round her grave I wander drear,
Noon, night, and morning early,
With breaking heart whene'er I hear
The wind that shakes the barley!

FANNY CLAIR.

Air—" Mōr Cluna".

I.

Queenly is thy mien and air,
Jewels sparkle in thy hair,
   And those ringlets twining,
   And thy dark eyes shining,
   Set my fond heart pining,
      Fanny Clair.

II.

Grace dwells in thy features fair,
Pride of birth sits haughty there,
   Yet in thy heart's glowing
   Love—on me bestowing
   Fond hopes brighter glowing,
      Fanny Clair.

III.

Never shall my heart despair
While that smile thy sweet lips wear:
   In it rests a token
   That thy love's awoken,
   Though it burns unspoken,
      Fanny Clair.

IV.

Then the life that else was bare
Shall find glory, spite of care,
   For thy sake shall never
   Cease each good endeavour,
   Till we're joined for ever,
      Fanny Clair!

WILLY BRAND.

Air—"Blow the candle out".

I.

My love is come of English blood,
    And was my father's foe;
But now he's all for Ireland's good
    As once for Ireland's woe;
And now he's leal and true as steel
    When war is in the land;
So aye through blame, and oh! through shame,
    I'll love my Willy Brand.

II.

My love he is a soldier free,
    So stately and so tall,
With armour shining gloriously,
    And sword, and plume, and all;
With horseman's shoon and musquetoon
    He rides by tower and strand,
And aye through blame, and oh! through shame,
    I'll love my Willy Brand.

III.

My love has drawn his gallant sword
    For Ireland's cause and king,
Black Cromwell with his blood-stained horde
    Of traitors back to fling;
And may God speed each man and steed
    The dark foe to withstand,
While aye through blame, and oh! through shame,
    I'll love my Willy Brand.

IV.

Each day she waited by the hill
   Her Willy Brand's return,
And still the same through woe and ill
   Her love for him did burn:
And back love gave her soldier brave
   When peace swayed o'er the land;
For aye through blame, and oh! through shame,
   She loved her Willy Brand!

THE LASSES OF IRELAND.

Air—"Pilib a Ceo".

I.

Here's to our dear lasses, wheresoe'er their home,
'Mid the ancient cities, or where wild streams foam;
Ne'er were hearts more constant, ne'er were eyes so bright,
So we'll pledge them fondly on this festive night.
    Then to our dear lasses,
      With their smiles divine,
    Drink, in sparkling glasses
      Of the rose-red wine!

II.

All the lovely maids that charmed our sires of yore,
Live and shine immortal in wild bardic lore;
Still the same sweet faces, still the forms so fair,
Bloom from Antrim's Pillars to the bright Kenmare.
    Then to those dear lasses,
      With their smiles divine,
    Drink, in sparkling glasses
      Of the rose-red wine!

III.

Once I was a rover through broad England's plains;
Through and through I've wandered Scotland's wild
    domains:
There I found fair maidens in the light of youth,
But no Irish fondness and no Irish truth.
        So to our own lasses,
           With their smiles divine,
        Drink, in sparkling glasses
           Of the rose-red wine!

IV.

Denmark's dames are lovely, with their locks of
    gold;
Spanish forms are stately; France hath charms un-
    told;
Yet that sweet, bright beauty filling glance and
    smile
Dwells but with the maidens of our own green isle.
        So to our own lasses,
           With their smiles divine,
        Drink, in sparkling glasses,
           Of the rose-red wine!

V.

May they live for ever as in th' olden time,
When brave warriors wooed them, and sweet bards
    sublime;
May their glorious faces shine for aye the same,
With the light of beauty and love's radiant flame!
        And to our own lasses,
           With their smiles divine,
        Drink, in sparkling glasses
           Of the rose-red wine!

O'SULLIVAN'S FLIGHT.

A.D. 1603.

Air—"Ca rouish anish an cailín vig".

I.

Glengariff's shore could give no more
 The shelter strong we needed,
So away we trode on our wintry road,
 Its dangers all unheeded.
   We'll shout hurra! for valour's sway,
    Each trembling coward scorning,
   For cleaving brands in dauntless hands,
    And all for freedom's morning!

II.

The snows were deep, the paths were steep,
 But worse than these soon found us—
The ruffian swords, and the traitor hordes
 That flocked like wolves around us!
   We'll shout hurra! etc.

III.

By Blarney's towers, Mac Caurha's powers
 Our good swords turned their backs on;
And Mallow's flood we stained with blood
 Of Barry, Rupe, and Saxon!
   Then shout hurra! etc.

IV.

By Gailty's hill around us still
 Rushed many a fierce marauder;
Yet our path we clave to Shannon's wave,
 And all by the good *lamh laider*.*
   Then shout hurra! etc.

---

* *Lamh láider*—the strong hand.

V.

Mac Eggan's wrath there barred our path,
    But we gave him warning early
To clear the way, or his bands we'd slay,
    And we kept our promise fairly!
        Then shout hurra! etc.

VI.

Each killed his steed in that hour of need,
    After false Mac Eggan's slaughter,
Corachs* unstaid of their skins we made,
    And crossed the Shannon's water!
        Then shout hurra! etc.

VII.

O'Sullivan was the dauntless man,
    When the foe by Aughrim found us,
Black Malby's head on the sward he laid,
    And we slew all around us!
        Then shout hurra! etc.

VIII.

Alas! how few of our brave and true
    Reached Ullad's† mountains hoary!
But none should weep for the brave who sleep
    On that path so rough and gory!
        But shout hurra! for valour's sway,
            Each trembling coward scorning,
        For cleaving brands in dauntless hands,
            And all for freedom's morning!

---

* *Corach*, a light boat. O'Sullivan ordered his men to cut osiers by the shore, and make boat frames of wickerwork. These frames they covered with the skins of their horses, and in the corachs or boats thus formed, they crossed the Shannon.

† *Ullad*—Ulster.

SONG.

Air—" The handsome face".

I.

A young bright face where all can trace
   The heart's pure thoughts ever shining there,
In dreamland golden there's nought beholden,
   Half so bewitching or half so fair.

II.

Two bright eyes like the summer skies,
   Where the soul laughs out in a living ray;
What can lighten the heart, and brighten
   Its depths, when darkened, so well as they?

III.

Lips as red as the light that's shed
   By the dew-bright roses in leafy June,
With the white teeth's splendour, and voice as tender,
   And soft and sweet as an old love tune.

IV.

Oh! my love, my maid of the wildwood glade
   In the western mountains, excels in all;
And through all ranging and fortune's changing,
   With those sweet charms keeps my heart in thrall!

THE STORMY SEA SHALL FLOW IN.

Air—"I wish I were an earl".

I.

The stormy sea shall flow in
   Our highland valleys through,
Ere I, my stately Owen,
   Prove false to love and you.
My heart was sad and lonely
   Each weary night and day,
And your kind accents only
   Could chase my grief away.

II.

For oh! my mother left me—
   Cold, cold in death she lies—
Ah! how drear fortune reft me
   Of all my heart could prize!
My father far would wander
   Unto some foreign zone,
And I was left to ponder
   Upon my grief alone!

III.

Then came a sure sweet token
   Such sorrows might not last,
The love in joy unspoken,
   You spoke when joy had passed;
Then, oh! the sea shall flow in
   Our highland valleys through,
Ere I, my stately Owen,
   Prove false to love and you!

MARGARET.

Air—"She is gone".

I.

The woods and the hills, and the flower-edged streams,
  Are brighter than they were wont to be,
For winter hath fled, and the sunny gleams
  Of spring-tide clothe them in radiancy;
But my Margaret is gone, and my golden dreams
  Are darkened and dead to me.

II.

All things look serene and bright—
  Crag and castle and vale and all—
The young lambs play in their fresh delight,
  And the sweet birds sing in the forest tall:
But my Margaret is gone, and the shades of night
  Dark down in my bosom fall.

III.

The clouds from the mountain tops have rolled,
  And the woods and the valleys are clad in green;
But where is she with the hair of gold,
  And the eyes so sweetly blue and sheen?
Ah! my Margaret is gone, and those dreams of old
  Shall never come back, I ween!

I LOVED A MAID.

Air—"The Rambling Sailor".

I.

I loved a maid by Geerait's lea,
  And knew by many a token
That love dwelt in her heart for me,
  Though long it lived unspoken;

I loved her well, I loved her true;
But she has crossed the ocean blue—
Yet can the links that fondly grew
    Thus round our hearts be broken?

II.

Ah! many a morn and starry night
    May sink down Time's dark river,
And youth may fade like all things bright,
    But nought our souls can sever;
For love shall live, the love of yore,
That filled our hearts by Geerait's shore,
Though angry oceans spread and roar
    Between us still for ever.

III.

There's many a maid 'neath Daragh's crest
    Whose fond love I might waken,
But never from my lonely breast
    Can thought of her be taken:—
I gaze on them, but constantly
Think, think on her beyond the sea:
Thus love and grief have dwelt with me,
    And ne'er my heart forsaken.

JESSY BRIEN.

Air—"As thro' the woods I chanced to rove".

I.

Jessy Brien! the livelong day,
    Down by Funcheon's river,
I think of her from June to May,
    Down by Funcheon's river;

I love her not for golden dower,
But oh! that she's the fairest flower
In lowly cot or lordly bower,
    Down by Funcheon's river.

II.

Ne'er were eyes so clear and blue,
    Down by Funcheon's river;
Ne'er was heart so good and true,
    Down by Funcheon's river;
And her long hair is so bright,
That it shines by day and night,
Like a cloud of golden light,
    Down by Funcheon's river.

III.

Within the chapel on the green,
    Down by Funcheon's river,
Oh! could you see my bosom's queen,
    Down by Funcheon's river,
Kneeling at the Sunday prayer,
She looks so bright and lovely there,
You'd deem she was an angel fair,
    Down by Funcheon's river!

IV.

And I will love my maiden mild,
    Down by Funcheon's river,
While lasts the water's song so wild,
    Down by Funcheon's river;
And sweetly as that fairy song,
While blest with love so true and strong,
Our lives in joy shall glide along,
    Down by Funcheon's river.

JOHNNY'S RETURN.

Air—"In comes a croppy".

I.

As Johnny came full merrily
  By Mona's ancient tower,
He saw his true love drearily
  Sit in the wild ash bower;
He spoke to her full cheerily,
  But aye she made her moan:
    "Oh! I'm left to weep all drearily
      My misery alone,
    For he whose words fell merrily
      On my poor heart is flown!"

II.

"When winter blasts were roaring wild,
  My love left me to weep;
And ere the larks were soaring wild,
  He'd crossed the stormy deep".
Then Johnny spoke full merrily,
  But aye she made her moan:
    "Oh! I'm left to weep all drearily
      My misery alone,
    For he whose words fell cheerily
      On my poor heart is flown!"

III.

Oh! dead her young heart's gladness then
  For two long weary years,
And wild she wailed her sadness then,
  And fast fell down her tears;
Yet Johnny spoke full merrily,
  But aye she made her moan:
    "Oh! I'm left to weep all drearily
      My misery alone,
    For he whose words fell cheerily
      On my poor heart is flown!"

IV.

He'd come disguised full drearily
   On his returning day;
With laugh and fond word, cheerily,
   He cast it now away;
He ran where Eileen drearily
   Sat making her sad moan:
     And merrily, oh! merrily,
      His arms were round her thrown,
   Crying, "Joy is dawning cheerily,
     And sorrow's night is flown!"

THE FORSAKEN.

Air—"The Gaddhe Gráine".

I.

The flowers are blooming by stream and fountain,
   The wild birds sing with a joyous tone,
And gladness gushes o'er vale and mountain,
   But I am left to my grief alone—
To wail alone in love's deep devotion,
   For young Dunlevy of the raven hair,
Has left his mountains, and crossed the ocean,
   To fight for France and for glory there.

II.

They tell me that his love is burning
   For me as fond as e'er it has been,
But when, ah! when comes his sweet returning
   To Erin's hills and his dark Eileen?

They tell me one sweet pleasant story,—
    My young Dunlevy's brave pride and joy,
When he had won the bright meed of glory,
    A captain's sabre at Fontenoy!

III.

The foreign maidens could ne'er have bound him
    In love's bright fetters, though fair they be,—
Yet ah! he comes not, though fame has found him,
    And well I love him and he loves me;
Alas! their vengeance is not half taken
    Upon the Saxon for his tyrannie,
And oh! how long shall I sit forsaken
    To wail alone by the murmuring sea?

I WISH I SAT BY GRENA'S SIDE.

Air—"I wish I had the yellow cow".

I.

I wish I sat by Grena's side
With the friends of boyhood-tide,
With the maids, the brilliant-eyed,
    Playful, wild, and airy,
Who taught me that love could go
Worship bright eyes to and fro,
But turning with fonder glow
    Back to you, my Mary!

II.

I wish I sat by Grena's stream,
In the ruddy sunset beam,
Where the waves leap, glance, and gleam,
    On through dell and wildwood;

Ne'er half so fleet and free,
As the fairy feet of glee
Which danced 'neath the summer tree
  In our dreamy childhood.

III.

I wish I sat by Grena's shore
With the green boughs waving o'er,
Where the glens and mountains hoar
  Shine, one land of faery;
Then, oh! how I'd muse and dream
Long beside that haunted stream,
And all on one golden theme,—
  You, my lovely Mary!

IV.

I wish I sat by Grena's wave,
Hopes fulfilled that boyhood gave,
Where the woods clothe gorge and cave,
  Storied hill and plain, love;
You placed beside me there,
Laughing, loving, wildly fair,
Long parted, lost, but ne'er,
  Ne'er to part again, love!

ROVING BRIAN O'CONNELL.

Air—"How do you like her for your wife?"

I.

"How do you like her for your wife,
  Roving Brian O'Connell?
A loving mate and true for life,
  Roving Brian O'Connell?"

"She's as fit to be my wife
As my sword is for the strife",
Said the Rapparee trooper,
    Roving Brian O'Connell!

II.

"Ne'er to Mabel prove untrue,
    Roving Brian O'Connell,
For oh! she'd die for love of you
    Roving Brian O'Connell!"
"Oh! my wild heart never knew
A flame so constant too",
Said the Rapparee trooper,
    Roving Brian O'Connell!

III.

"Never man my child will take,
    Roving Brian O'Connell,
Save him who'd die for Ireland's sake,
    Roving Brian O'Connell".
"Oh! I'd die for Ireland's sake,
And her bonds we soon will break!"
Said the Rapparee trooper,
    Roving Brian O'Connell!

IV.

"Her father died, as dies the brave,
    Roving Brian O'Connell,
Beneath the blow the Saxon gave,
    Roving Brian O'Connell".
"Next we'll meet the Saxon knave,
He'll get pike and gun and glaive!"
Said the Rapparee trooper,
    Roving Brian O'Connell.

V.

"How will you your young bride keep,
　Roving Brian O'Connell?
The foeman's bands are ne'er asleep,
　Roving Brian O'Connell".
"In our hold by Conail's steep
Who dare make my Mabel weep?"
Said the Rapparee trooper,
　Rvving Brian O'Connell.

VI.

"This day in ruined church you stand,
　Roving Brian O'Connell,
To take your young bride's priceless hand,
　Roving Brian O'Connell"—
"Oh, my heart, my arm, and brand,
Are for her and our dear land!"
Said the Rapparee trooper,
　Roving Brian O'Connell!

THE ADVICE.

Air—"The advice".

I.

Redmond spoke the wise old man,—
　Redmond Clare of Corrin's highland,—
"Oh! win my maid I never can,
　The proudest heart in Erin's island;

Day by day I've gone to woo,
   And found but pride and black displeasure!"
Then said the sage, "If love won't do,
   Go court her all with golden treasure".

II.

Redmond was the comeliest man
   From Brandon hill to Barrow's water,
Yet high howe'er his passion ran,
   She frowned on all the love he brought her;
And Redmond came of gentle kin,
   But ah! he lacked fair Fortune's measure,
And when he failed her heart to win,
   'Twas but for want of golden treasure.

II.

To foreign climes he never ran,
   But wrought within his native island,
Until at last the richest man
   In all the glens of Corrin's highland.
He went to woo the maid again,
   And met all smiles and courtly pleasure,
And found, proud woman's heart to win,
   There's nothing like the golden treasure!

THE FLAME THAT BURNED SO BRIGHTLY.

Air—"Saddle the Pony".

I.

There was a light in the window pane,
   Still burning, brightly burning,
And it gleamed afar over Cleena's main,
   On Donall's bark returning;

And he looked up, the cliffs between,
    Where the hamlet glimmered nightly,
And thought he saw his own Kathleen,
    By the flame that burned so brightly.

II.

It was upon All-Hallow's night,
    When the candles bright were burning,
That the beams fell from that constant light,
    On Donall's bark returning;
It lit like a star the darkening scene,
    And made his heart beat lightly,
For he thought he saw his own Kathleen,
    By the flame that burned so brightly.

III.

He moored his bark the hamlet near,
    Where the candles bright were burning,
But a mournful wail met his startled ear,
    All Hallows night returning;
And he heard a name in that piercing keen,
    And saw a shroud gleam whitely—
'Twas the waking light of his own Kathleen,
    The flame that burned so brightly!

EILEEN'S LAMENT FOR GERALD.

Air—"Slan lath a chur".

I.

By loud Avondhu
While the sweet flowerets blew,
I've mourned for my Gerald the long summer through,
    And autumn falls lone
    On Kilmore's mountain zone,
But Cleena, still Cleena ne'er heedeth my moan!

II.

Oh! sweet fell the hours
By Crom's lordly towers,
When we strayed, ever loving, through Maig's blooming bowers—
From bright June to May,
Was our blissful day,
Ere my true love was borne from his Eileen away.

III.

With gems of red gold
Gleamed his mail in the wold,
As he slept where the lone Druid worshipped of old;
But the young Fairy Queen
Passed there in the e'en,
And the flash of his bright mail was never more seen!

IV.

She bore him that night
To her palace of light,
In this rock wild and lone, by the spells of her might,
And she keeps him in thrall,
The bright Prince of her hall,
While she heeds not my wailing, and hears not my call.

V.

And thus I must weep
By Cleena's gray steep,
Joy faded, hope clouded, and sorrow more deep;
Yet firmer and true
To the one love I knew,
Till I die in my sorrow by loud Avondhu!

MY TRUE LOVE.

Air—"The May Morning".

I.

My love has a form of splendour;
  My love has an eye divine;
My love has a heart full tender,
  And I know that heart is mine;
Her swan-like neck and bosom
  Are softly fair and pure
As the snowy wild-rose blossom,
  Or the white flower of the moor.

II.

The summer streamlets playing,
  Flow down in light and song,
So my thoughts to her go straying
  Through night and all day long,
And to the bliss which crowned me,
  When I kissed her o'er and o'er,
When my true love's arms were round me
  By the wild lake's rocky shore.

III.

My love's like a bright May morning,
  So pure, so mild, so bland;
My love's like a rose adorning
  A bower in some fairy land;—
How I long for red eve's shining,
  To see my true love stand,
Her golden tresses twining
  With her snow-white lily hand!

IV.

There's a stream in the wildwood springing,
  Where the birds chant on each tree:
Oh! I deem them for ever singing,
  My mountain maid, of thee!

And that stream the mountains blue, love,
   A deep sea shall o'erflow,
Ere I forsake my true love,
   Or my heart one change shall know.

SONG OF SARSFIELD'S TROOPER.

AIR—"Here's our brave Lord Lucan".

I.

The night fell dark on Limerick, and all the land
   was still,
As for the foe in ambush we lay beside the hill—
Like lions bold we waited to rush upon our prey,
With noble Sarsfield at our head, before the break
   of day.
From Dublin came the foeman with guns and war-
   like store—
To gain the walls of Limerick he'd want full ten
   times more;
And little was he dreaming that there to work his
   doom,
We'd come with gallant Sarsfield, far down from
   wild Sliav Bluim.

II.

At the lonely hour of midnight each man leapt on
   his steed,
And 'cross the bridge of Cullen we dashed with lightning speed,
And up the way we thundered to Ballineety's wall,
Where lay our foes securely with guns and stores
   and all!

When they asked for the password, "Ho! Sarsfield is the man!
And here I am!" our General cried, as down on them we ran;
Then God He cleared the firmament, the moon and stars gave light,
And for the battle of the Boyne we had revenge that night!*

III.

When we'd slain them all, brave Sarsfield he bade us take that store
Of baggage-carts, and powder, and arms and guns galore,
And pile them by the castle, and place the fuse full nigh;
And that we did right speedily, and blew them in the sky!
How pleasant spoke our General as fast we rode away!
And many a health we drank to him in Limerick next day;
Here's another health to Sarsfield, who led us one and all,
And took the foe's artillery by Ballineety's wall!

THE WANDERER.
Air—"Slan Beo".

I.

Oh! sweet are the woods that circle my Helen's wild home,
Oh! sweetest her smiles from Houra to Cleena's bright foam,

---

* These two lines are from an old song on the same subject, the fragments of which remain still among the peasantry.

And brightest her eyes 'mong the blue eyes of splendour that beam
'Mid the hills of the South, by wildwood and fountain and stream.

II.

I sat all alone by the wood-screened banks of the Suir,
While the calm sky of eve shone bright in its breast fresh and pure—
Oh! every fair cloud like a gold-winged angel above,
Left an image below—a glory-robed trace of my love.

III.

And once by the marge of Cleena's waters I lay,
In a sweet dream of love and joy at the opening of day;
The beams of the morn smiled over the blue billows there,
The smiles of my love, the wreaths of her long golden hair.

IV.

By Shannon's green shore my wandering footsteps I stayed
On a wave-worn steep, to dream of my yellow-haired maid;
I thought of her archéd brow and fair neck of snow,
As I saw the fleet wing of the white gull gleaming below.

V.

And thus as I stray by river and wildwood and sea,
All nature still paints but one lovely image for me,
And oh! for the joy when standing by Ounanar's tide,
In the greenwood again with my bright-eyed love by my side.

FAIREST AND RAREST.

Air—"The rarest maid".

I.

Fairest and rarest
  Of all the maids that be,
Sweetest, and meetest
  For minstrel's love is she,
She who loved me longest,
  When far, far away;—
With a love the strongest
  I love her to-day!

II.

Keep me and steep me
  In black sorrow's wave,
Fair dreams and rare dreams
  Of my love could save;—
Save my heart, and borrow
  Light in such dark doom,
Make, 'mid desert sorrow,
  Joy's gay flowers to bloom.

III.

Deeming, sweet dreaming,
  Such a joy to me,
How bright with joy's light
  Must the present be!
When her eyes are shining,
  Void of care and pain,
When her arms are twining
  Round me once again!

COME, ALL YOU MAIDS, WHERE'ER YOU BE.

Air—"Come, all you maids".

I.

Come, all you maids, where'er you be,
   That flourish fair and fine, fine,
To young and old I will unfold
   This hopeless tale of mine,
          Mine,
   This hopeless tale of mine!

II.

The sun shall set upon my grief,
   The sun shall rise the same, same,
And ever so shall live my woe
   Enduring as his flame,
          Flame,
   Enduring as his flame.

III.

My home was in the border land,
   Where the flashing streams rush down, down,
From Houra's hill; there with gallant Will
   I met in the autumn brown,
          Brown,
   I met in the autumn brown.

IV.

He said, his love so fond and true
   Would never die for me, me,
That my eyes shamed the hue of the violet blue,
   And my lips the red rose tree,
          Tree,
   The bloom of the red rose tree.

V.

Alas! I liked and loved him well,
    Though I answered cold as stone, stone,
So he turned his steed to the wars with speed,
    And he left me weeping lone,
            Lone,—
    To sigh and weep alone.

VI.

Grief made my love burn wild and strong,
    So I followed him full fain, fain,
But by Knock'noss Hill, oh! my gallant Will
    Lay dying amid the slain,
            Slain,
    Lay dying amid the slain!

VII.

And down I knelt by my true-love's side,
    And he bent his eyes on me, me;
One long, long look of love he took,
    And he died on that blood-stained lea,
            Lea,
    He died on that blood-stained lea!

VIII.

The sun shall set upon my grief,
    The sun shall rise the same, same,
And ever so shall live my woe,
    Enduring as his flame,
            Flame,
    Enduring as his flame!*

---

* From the fragments of an old song on the same subject, and in the same metre.

MARY, THE PRIDE OF THE WEST.

Air—"Nancy, the pride of the east".

I.

The summer shines bright from the plain
    To the hills where the gray rocks are piled;
The birds sing a clear, joyous strain,
    And the flowers are in bloom o'er the wild;
But a flower, all these fair flow'rs above
    In sweetness, blooms deep in my breast;
'Tis the lone flower of fondness and love
    For Mary, the Pride of the West.

II.

There's an ash-tree that blooms light and fair,
    Where the linnets in May make their bower;
There's a rose-bush beyond all compare,
    By the walls of the gray mountain tower;
But how lovely soe'er that lone tree,
    And the bush all in white blossoms drest,
As fair and as lovely is she,
    My Mary, the Pride of the West.

III.

When she goes from the wild hills among
    To the town on the verge of the plain,
Could you see her sweet face 'mid the throng,
    You ne'er would forget it again;
And the gallants who pass, when they see,
    And the crowd, think her brightest and best,
And they ask who such fair maid can be,
    My Mary, the Pride of the West!

IV.

When each night at her father's broad hearth
    I sit near my love by the fire,
I have all that my heart on this Earth
    Can love, and adore, and admire;
Then her eyes, like two clear stars above,
    With their kind looks on me often rest,
'Till I'm wild, wild with fondness and love
    For Mary, the Pride of the West!

MY LOVE IS ON THE RIVER.

Air—"Ta mo grad sa ar an abainn".

I.

Sliav Gua's highlands shade meadow and moor,
And guard the green islands of the golden Suir:
The Tar brightly sallies from their cooms, wild and fleet,
And sings through the valleys that bloom at their feet.
More bright to-day than they e'er shone before,
Shine castle gray, and green height, and shore,—
Oh! the splendours that quiver o'er wildwood and lea,
While my love is on the river in his light boat with me!

II.

Swift as foot of the beagle from the hills doth he hie;
Bright as glance of the eagle, the glance of his eye;

When the Green Flag's unfurled he is straight as its
    tree,
Never heart in the world could be fonder of me.
Outlawed and lone lived he many a day,
In his cold cave of stone 'mid the hills far away;
But truth conquers ever, and my love he is free
On the Suir's golden river in his light boat with me!

III.

Sweet songs are ringing from the birds of the grove,
But sweeter the singing of my own gallant love:
Oh! his brave words first found me in sadness and
    pain,
But they soon strewed around me joy's bright flow'rs
    again.
And he never more from my arms shall be torn,
The fair chapel door shall receive us next morn;
And the green woods shall quiver to our bridal bell's
    glee,
For my love is on the river in his light boat with me!

GLENARA.

Air—"She is my true love".

I.

Grand are the mountains that circle Glenara,
See-Fein, wild Corrin, Cnoc Aodh, and Sliav Dara;
Proudly their summits look down where its sheen
    flood
Lies coiled in the gorges, or sunk in the greenwood.

II.

Sweet are the scenes where that wild flood enlarges,
Peaceful the homes by its flower-scented marges;
Fair are the maidens with eyes brightly glowing,
Who bide by its windings and list to its flowing.

III.

Ever the fairest 'mid beauty's gay daughters,
Dwells my young love by the sound of its waters;
Roams she at eve through its fairy recesses,
My maid of the blue eyes and long golden tresses.

IV.

One summer even I sped to the fountain—
Sped to her side from my home o'er the mountain;
There a lone dreamer to sweet bliss awoken,
My fond vows of love to a fond heart were spoken.

V.

Far from my dear mountain home as I wander,
Ever with joy on that evening I ponder,
Thinking and dreaming how fraught with sweet glory
My days by her side 'mid those hills wild and hoary.

MARGREAD BAN.

Air—"The old astrologer".

I.

My wild heart's love, my woodland dove,
    The tender and the true,
She dwells beside a blue stream's tide
    That bounds through wild Glenroe;
Through every change her love's the same—
    A long bright summer dawn—
A gentle flame—and oh! her name
    Is lovely Margréad Bān—
Oh! joy, that on her paths I came,
    My lovely Margréad Bān.

II.

When winter hoar comes freezing o'er
    The mountains wild and gray,
Her neck is white as snow-wreaths bright,
    Upon thy crags, Cnoc Aodh;
Her lips are red as roses sweet
    On Dara's flowery lawn;
Her fairy feet are light and fleet,
    My gentle Margréad Bān;
And oh! her steps I love to meet,
    My own dear Margréad Bān.

III.

When silence creeps o'er Houra's steeps,
    As blue eve ends its reign,
Her long lock's fold is like the gold
    That gleams o'er sky and main.
My heart's fond sorrow fled away
    Like night before the dawn,
When one spring day I went astray,
    And met my Margréad Bān,
And felt her blue eyes' sparkling ray,—
    My lovely Margaret Bán.

V.

One summer noon, to hear the tune
    Of wild birds in the wood,
Where murmuring streams flashed back the beams,
    All wrapt in bliss I stood;
The birds sang from the fairy moat,
    From greenwood, brake, and lawn;
But never throat could chant a note
    So sweet as Margréad Bān,
As through the vales her wild songs float,
    My lovely Margréad Bān!

V.

Oh! would that we for love might flee
    To some far valley green,
Where never more by rock or shore
    Dark sorrow could be seen.
I know a valley wildly fair,
    From strife far, far withdrawn;
And ever there the loving air
    Of gentle Margréad Bān
Would keep this fond heart free from care,
    My lovely Margréad Bān!

ASTHOREEN MACHREE.

Air—"Astorin Machree".

I.

Summer with gay flowers the hills was adorning,
    Streams through the wildwood sang sweetly and free,
As I 'scaped from my cell at the dawn of the morning,
    My dark tyrant scorning, Asthoreen Machree!

II.

Oh! in that prison my heart was all sadness!
    Oh! but the long days fell heavy on me,
Still thinking I never might see thee in gladness,
    Brooding in madness, Asthoreen Machree!

III.

Now I have 'scaped, but such darkness was never;
    How could the brightness arise save from thee?
Woe and despair they have crossed my endeavour—
    Thou sleeping for ever, Asthoreen Machree!

IV.

Out in the forest the branches are shaking;
   There the sad Banshee is wailing for me;
Down from the trees the strong boughs she is taking,
   My bier she is making, Asthoreen Machree!

V.

Soon shall we meet in the grave's silent dwelling;
   Oh! but 'tis joy thus to slumber with thee—
Soon shall the keeners my hard fate be telling,
   My death-bell loud knelling, Asthoreen Machree!

OVER THE HILLS AND FAR AWAY.

AIR—" Over the hills".

I.

From night till morn, from morn till night,
My thoughts dwell with a sweet delight,
And all upon a maiden bright
Who dwells by Houra's rocky height,
      Over the hills and far away,
      Over the hills and far away,
      I think of her both night and day,
      Over the hills and far away.

II.

And is my maid a proper theme?
And is she worthy of my dream?
Go, catch her smile and clear eyes' beam,
By Houra's hill or Grena's stream,
      Over the hills and far away,
      And ne'er was one, you'll think and say,
      So lovely as my maiden gay,
      Over the hills and far away.

III.

And have you seen the violet blow?
Its tints within her fond eyes glow;
Her skin is fair as blooms that grow,
In wild March in the fragrant sloe,
      Over the hills and far away,
      Over the hills and far away,
      I think of her both night and day,
      Over the hills and far away.

IV.

Yet 'tis not for her sweet smile's charm,
And 'tis not for her graceful form,
But for her heart so true and warm,
My love burns on through calm and storm.
      Over the hills and far away,
      Whate'er my lot, where'er I stray,
      I'll think of her both night and day,
      Over the hills and far away!

THE WITHERED ROSE.
Air—"The Orange Rogue".

I.

Fair blooms array the summer bowers
    Along the woodlands airy,
But fairer still this flower of flowers
    I got from my dear Mary.
The purple heath-bell paints the steep,
    Wild rock and glen illuming;
More dear this withered flower I keep,
    Than all the wild flowers blooming.
      Oh! fair the blooms that deck the bowers,
        And paint the mountains airy,
      Oh! fairer still this flower of flowers,
        I got from my dear Mary!

II.

Oh! sweet the days of long ago,
    When love with joy was weaven,
When in the fairy dells below
    We met each summer even;
When Mary sat in beauty nigh,
    And sang the songs I taught her,
And spoke the love that ne'er shall die,
    By Grena's sunny water.
        Oh! fair the blooms that deck the bowers,
            And paint the mountains airy!
        Oh! fairer still this flower of flowers
            I got from my dear Mary!

III.

It was upon a Saint John's night
    She gave me that red blossom;
'Twas blooming in its freshness bright
    Upon her loving bosom;
And since, through changing joys and tears,
    Though fate her smiles denied me—
Oh! ever since, for five long years,
    I've kept that flower beside me!
        Oh! sweet the blooms that deck the bowers,
            And paint the mountains airy!
        Oh! sweeter still this flower of flowers,
            I got from my dear Mary.

IV.

And when once more I meet her gaze
    By Grena's crystal water,
How sweet to talk of those young days
    When by the wave I sought her;
When care is fled, and woe is dead,
    And joy alone is shining,
When meeting then in that wild glen,
    Her arms are round me twining;

Oh! then beside our native bowers,
  Amid the woodlands airy,
This long-kept, priceless flower of flowers
  I'll show to my dear Mary!

THE JOY-BELLS.

Air—"The bells of Barna".

I.

Blithesome is our marriage morn,
  Blithesome are our hearts and gay,
Though in no high carriage borne,
  Though we've neither pomp nor sway;
And the joy-bells' constant ringing
  Floats upon the mountain wind,
Ringing, ringing, sweetly bringing
  Many a glad thought to my mind.
    O the joy-bells! O the joy-bells!
      Ringing, ringing sweet and clear,
    In the May-time of our loving
      And the May-tide of the year!

II.

This small chapel by the mountain
  For our bridal's fittest place,
With its fairy thorn and fountain,
  And its old familiar face;
With the gray priest vested meekly,
  Like a saint from Heaven above;
With our parents smiling sweetly
  On our fond and deathless love.

O the joy-bells! O the joy-bells!
   Ringing, ringing sweet and clear,
In the May-time of our loving
   And the May-tide of the year!

III.

Once the golden *Mi na Meala*,*
   With its sunny hours is o'er,
Grief may come, but joy must follow
   When I pass my husband's door;
For my Donall loves me kindly,
   And though love the judgment dim,
'Twas but slow, and 'tis not blindly
   That I gave my heart to him.
   O the joy-bells! O the joy-bells!
      Ringing, ringing, sweet and clear,
   In the May-time af our loving,
      And the May-tide of the year.

JOHNNY DUNLEA.

Air—"Johnny Dunlea".

I.

There's a tree in the greenwood I love best of all—
It stands by the side of Easmore's haunted fall—
For there while the sunset shone bright far away
Last I met 'neath its branches my Johnny Dunlea.

II.

Oh! to see his fine form as he rode down the hill,
While the red sunset glowed on his helmet of steel;
With his broadsword and charger so gallant and
   gay,
On that evening of woe for my Johnny Dunlea.

---

* The Honeymoon.

III.

He stood by my side, and the love smile he wore
Still brightens my heart, though 'twill beam never
    more,
'Twas to have but one farewell, then speed to the fray,
'Twas a farewell for ever, my Johnny Dunlea!

IV.

For the red Saxon soldiers lay hid in the dell,
And burst on our meeting with wild savage yell:
But their leader's black life-blood I saw that sad day,
And it stained the good sword of my Johnny Dunlea!

V.

My curse on the traitors, my curse on the ball
That stretched my true-love by Easmore's haunted
    fall;
Oh! the blood of his brave heart ebbed quickly
    away,
And he died in my arms there, my Johnny Dunlea!

THE JOLLY COMPANIE.

Air—"The jolly companie".

I.

Oh! we are jolly soldiers
    Of courage stout and true,
Some in strife grown hoary
    And some to battle new.
We're going to the wars
    Beyond the Irish sea,
Our green flag o'er us waving,
    A jolly companie!
    A jolly companie!
    A jolly companie!
In bivouac, or wild attack,
    A jolly companie!

II.

When we sailed from the harbour,
    Our hearts were sad and sore
For the girls we left behind us
    Upon the Irish shore :—
Though the girls in France are fair,
    To our own still true we'll be,
As we fight our way to glory,
    A jolly companie!
    A jolly companie!
    A jolly companie!
Around the can, or man to man,
    A jolly companie!

III.

Here's a health to good King Lewis,
    Our friend for evermore,
And a health to poor Righ Shamus,
    May his troubles soon be o'er,—
Where'er the pike we trail
    We'll smite his enemie
To the tune of "Fág an bealach",
    A jolly companie!
    A jolly companie!
    A jolly companie!
In peace or fight, by day or night,
    A jolly companie!

IV.

When we look upon our flag-staff
    Of the hardy Irish oak,
'Twill remind us of our country
    'Mid the battle's dust and smoke ;—

In danger's stormy gap,
  Our gory bed may be,
But we'll die like sons of Ireland,
    A jolly companie!
    A jolly companie!
    A jolly companie!
In bivouac or wild attack,
    A jolly companie!

THE FIRST NIGHT I WAS MARRIED.*

Air—"The first night I was married".

I.

The first night I was married and made a happy bride,
The captain of the cavalry he came to my bed side:
"Arise, arise, new married man,—arise, and come with me,
To the lowlands of Holland to face your enemie!

II.

Holland is a pretty place, the fairest I have seen,
With the way-sides glittering all in flowers, and the fields so bright and green;
The sunshine lights the clustering grapes, where the vines hang from each tree!"
And I scarce had time to look about when my true love was gone from me!

---

* From the fragments of an old song sung by the peasantry of Limerick.

III.

Oh! weeping, weeping sorely, I waste each day and night,
Thinking of the hours I spent with my own heart's delight:
My curse upon the cruel wars that drove him o'er the sea,
To the lowlands of Holland, far, far away from me!

IV.

I built my love a gallant ship to bear him o'er the main,
With four-and-twenty sailors bold, all for a fitting train;
The storm came down upon the sea, and the waves began to roar,
And dashed my love and his gallant ship upon the Holland shore!

V.

Says the mother to the daughter, "What makes you so lament?
Is there no man in green Ireland to please your discontent?"
"There are men enough in green Ireland, but none at all for me,
For I never loved but one young man, now far beyond the sea!"

VI.

I'll build my love another ship, and give its sails the wind,
And search among the bold Brigade my gallant love to find;
I'll search among the bold Brigade, with heart full fond and fain,
And I'll bring back my true love from the wild, wild wars again!

THE BRIGADE'S HURLING MATCH.*

Air—" The game played in Erinn go Bragh".

I.

In the South's blooming valleys they sing and they play,
By their vine-shaded cots at the close of the day;
But a game like our own the Brigade never saw—
The wild, sweeping hurlings of Erinn go Bragh.

II.

Our tents they were pitched upon Lombardy's plain;
Ten days nigh the foeman our army had lain;
But ne'er through his towers made we passage or flaw,
Till we showed them the game played in Erinn go Bragh.

III.

Our sabres were sharp, and a forest was nigh,
There our hurleys we fashioned ere morning rose high;
With the goal-ball young Mahon had brought from Dunlawe,
We showed them the game played in Erinn go Bragh.

IV.

Our captain stood out with the ball in his hand;
Our colonel he gave us the word of command;
Then we dashed it and chased it o'er esker and scragh,
While we showed them the game played in Erinn go Bragh.

---

* This story is told among the people of Cork and Limerick.

V.

The enemy stood on their walls high and strong,
  While we raced it, and chased it, and dashed it along;
And they opened their gates as we nearer did draw,
To see the wild game played in Erinn go Bragh.

VI.

We left the round ball in its roaring career,
We turned on the foe with a wild ringing cheer—
Ah! they ne'er through our bright dauntless stratagem saw,
  While we showed them the game played in Erinn go Bragh!

VII.

Their swords clashed around us, their balls raked us sore,
But with hurleys we payed them in hard knocks galore;
For their bullets and sabres we cared ne'er a straw
While we showed them the game played in Erinn go Bragh.

VIII.

The fortress is taken, our wild shouts arise,
For our land and King Lewis they swell to the skies—
Ah! he laughed as he told us a game he ne'er saw
Like the wild, sweeping hurlings of Erinn go Bragh!

MY IRISH GIRL.

Air—"Costly were the robes of gold this Irish girl did wear".

I.

My Irish girl is young and fair
    With lightsome eyes of blue,
With guileless heart and modest air,
    And lips of red rose hue.
I met my love the plains above,
    Amid the hills so free,
And evermore think o'er and o'er
    The vows she made to me.

II.

I think within my lonely room—
    I think of Mary dear,
Till sunny bloom lights up the gloom,
    And she seems smiling near.
My heart's dear pearl, my Irish girl,
    Thy words so fond to me,
Have filled my breast with visions blest,
    And deathless love for thee.

III.

Beside me stands the lonely chair
    Where thou didst sit that night,
With loving air and face as fair,
    And eyes like wells of light;
That seat so lone, than golden throne
    Is far more dear to me,
For in my dream by firelight gleam
    Thy form still there I see.

IV.

Oh! fond, oh! fond my heart doth beat,
    And wild with dear delight,
When I think on the kisses sweet
    You gave to me that night.
My heart's dear pearl, my Irish girl,
    Love shines full constantly—
Howe'er it burn, a fond return
    It meets, my love, from thee!

ADIEU, LOVELY MARY.

Air—"Adieu, lovely Mary".

I.

"Adieu, lovely Mary—I'm going to leave you,
    And to the West Indies my sad course to steer,
I know very well my long absence will grieve you,
    But I will be back in the spring of the year!"

II.

The May-fires were burning, and ships were returning,
    But word never came to allay her sad fear,
And sorely and sadly young Mary sat mourning
    The loss of her love in the spring of the year.

III.

And summer thus found her, and wooers came round her,
    Yet deep in her bosom one form she held dear,—
She answered them weeping, "My love I am keeping
    For one who'll be back in the spring of the year!"

IV.

The old man with treasure, the young man with
    pleasure,
  Still courted till autumn was yellow and sear;
No fond vows were broken, the same words were
    spoken,
  "My love will be back in the spring of the year!"

V.

Next spring flowers were shining, and Mary sat
    twining
  A wreath of their blooms, and her heart was not
    drear,
For oh! with love glowing, when soft winds were
    blowing,
  Her true love came back in the spring of the
    year!

I'M FOURTEEN YEARS OLD UPON SUNDAY.*
Air—"As I went a walking".

I.

Adown by the Suir, in a May morning's shine,
I saw a young maiden a milking her kine;
And she sang, "Oh! my bosom no more shall re-
    pine,
  For I'm fourteen years old upon Sunday,
  And I shall be married on Sunday!"

II.

"Oh! love is the fondest the day it is new,
And the heart is a rover, and often untrue,
And will he be fonder, the bridegroom of you,
  But fourteen years old upon Sunday,
  And after your wedding on Sunday?"

---

* Partly an old song.

III.

"I know him too truly, my brave Conor Lee!
His mind from all thoughts of a rover is free,
And I'm sure in my heart he'll be fonder of me,
    But fourteen years old upon Sunday,
    And after our wedding on Sunday!

IV.

"On Saturday night I'll be void of all care,
With my new bridal dress and the flowers in my hair,
With three pretty maidens to wait on me there,
    And to dance at my wedding on Sunday,
    For I shall be married on Sunday!"

THE SUMMER IS COME.

Air—"The summer is come".

I.

The summer is come and the grass is green,
The gay flowers spring where the snows have been,
The ships are sailing upon the sea,
And I'll soon get tidings of Gra Machree.

II.

Oh! weary, weary, the long dull night
I think and think of my heart's delight,
And in my dreamings constantly
See the stately form of my Gra Machree.

III.

The birds are singing from brake and bough,
And sweetly, sweetly remind me now,
The day we danced by the village tree
When I won the heart of my Gra Machree.

IV.

I'm sure, I'm sure, while the sunbeams glow,
While flowers are springing and soft winds blow,
The white ships sailing upon the sea
Will soon bring tidings of Gra Machree.

OVER THE MORNING DEW.

Air—" As truagh gan peata vier agum".

I.

It is the sweetest hour for love :
The sun is o'er the eastern grove,
And nought is heard but coo of dove,
    And wild streams in the greenwood ; —
Over the morning dew,
Over the morning dew,
Come with me, young Gra Machree,
    Unto the leafy greenwood !

II.

With flowers that bloom so sweetly there
I'll deck thy dress and golden hair,
And thou hast never looked so fair,
    As there in that wild greenwood ; —
Over the morning dew,
Over the morning dew,
Come with me, young Gra Machree,
    Unto the leafy greenwood !

III.

There rears the Rath its lonely height,
Where fairies dance at noon of night,
And there my faith I'll fondly plight
    To thee in that wild greenwood!
Over the morning dew,
Over the morning dew,
Come with me, young Gra Machree,
    Unto the leafy greenwood!

IV.

Oh! fear not here to stray with me;
You know me from your infancy;
I'll ask but look of love from thee,
    And fond kiss in the greenwood.
Over the morning dew,
Over the morning dew,
Then come with me, young Gra Machree,
    Unto the leafy greenwood!

THE BOYS OF WEXFORD.*

Air—"The boys of Wexford".

I.

In comes the captain's daughter,—the captain of the Yeos,
Saying, "Brave United man, we'll ne'er again be foes.

---

* The fragments of an old song.

A thousand pounds I'll give you, and fly from home
    with thee,
And dress myself in man's attire, and fight for
    libertie!"
            We are the boys of Wexford, who fought
                with heart and hand
                To burst in twain the galling chain, and
                    free our native land!

II.

And when we left our cabins, boys, we left with
    right good will,
To see our friends and neighbours that were at
    Vinegar Hill;
A young man from our ranks a cannon he let go:
He slapt it into Lord Mountjoy—a tyrant he laid
    low!
            We are the boys of Wexford, who fought
                with heart and hand
                To burst in twain the galling chain, and
                    free our native land!

III.

We bravely fought and conquered at Ross, and
    Wexford town,
And if we failed to keep them, 'twas drink that
    brought us down.
We had no drink beside us on Tubber'neering's day,
Depending on the long bright pike, and well it
    worked its way!
            We are the boys of Wexford, who fought
                with heart and hand
                To burst in twain the galling chain, and
                    free our native land.

IV.

They came into the country our blood to waste and spill:
But let them weep for Wexford, and think of Oulart hill!
'Twas drink that still betrayed us,—of them we had no fear,
For every man could do his part like Forth and Shelmalier!
  We are the boys of Wexford, who fought with heart and hand
  To burst in twain the galling chain, and free our native land!

V.

My curse upon all drinking,—it made our hearts full sore,
For bravery won each battle, but drink lost evermore;
And if for want of leaders we lost at Vinegar hill,
We're ready for another fight, and love our country still!
  We are the boys of Wexford, who fought with heart and hand
  To burst in twain the galling chain, and free our native land!

SWEET GLENGARIFF'S WATER.

Air—" As I was riding out one day".

I.

Where wild fowl swim upon the lake
 At morning's early shining,
I'm sure, I'm sure my heart will break
 With sadness and repining.

As I went out one morning sweet,
   I met a farmer's daughter,
With gown of blue and milk-white feet,
   By sweet Glengariff's water.

II.

Her jet-black locks with wavy shine
   Fell sweetly on her shoulder,
And ah! they make my heart repine
   Till I again behold her;—
She smiled, and passed me strangely by,
   Though fondly I besought her;
And long I'll rue her laughing eye
   By sweet Glengariff's water.

III.

Where wild-fowl swim upon the lake
   At morning's early splendour,
Each day my lonely path I'll take,
   With thoughts full sad and tender;
I'll meet my love, and sure she'll stay
   To hear the tale I've brought her—
To marry me this merry May
   By sweet Glengariff's water.

AMONG THE FRAGRANT HAY.

Air—"Young Roger was a ploughboy".

I.

Young Johnnie, in the autumn,
   To Limerick he came,
And none could tell what brought him,
   And none could tell his name;

But he sat by Bessie Gray,
  That sunny autumn day,
And he told her sweet romances 'mid the new-mown hay.
      Then, oh! for fields lighted
        By sweet autumn's ray,
      When loving vows are plighted
        Among the fragrant hay!

II.

When ere the next sweet morning
  Young Johnnie had fled,
With envy filled and scorning,
  The village maidens said:
Oh! they spoke of Bessie Gray,
And they said she'd rue the day
When she heard the sweet romances 'mid the new-mown hay.
      Then, oh! for fields lighted
        By sweet autumn's ray,
      When loving vows are plighted
        Among the fragrant hay!

III.

Young Johnnie's happy dwelling
  Lay fast by the Lee,
And in manly parts excelling
  But few like him you'd see;
And so thought Bessie Gray
Since that lovely autumn day
When she heard the sweet-romances 'mid the new-mown hay.
      Then oh! for fields lighted
        By sweet autumn's ray,
      When loving vows are plighted
        Among the fragrant hay!

IV.

Young Johnnie could remember
  His vows and his flame,—
He came in dark December,
    And told his kin and name;
    And there was a wedding gay,
    And the bride was Bessie Gray,
And all from these romances 'mid the new-mown
    hay.
      Then, oh! for fields lighted
        By sweet autumn's ray
      When loving vows are plighted
        Among the fragrant hay!

THE SADDEST BREEZE.

AIR—"Johnnie, lovely Johnnie!"

I.

The saddest breeze in all the land,
  It blew across the sea;
It drove a brave ship from the strand,
  And bore my Hugh from me;
And long I sat beside the rill
  To weep my fate alone,
Till leaf and flower from wood and hill
  With summer beams were flown.

II.

The gladdest breeze e'er swept the vales
  To-day blew from the sea;
It swelled a good ship's snowy sails,
  And brought him back to me;

And now 'tis rushing wildly past,
　With wintry sleet and rain,
Yet e'en I love the cold, cold blast
　That brought my Hugh again!

MY LOVE IS AT MY SIDE.

Air—" I once loved a boy".

I.

The lone hill's dells are blue with heather bells,
　The wild flowers bloom along the moor,
The soft winds glide, and my love is at my side,
　On the banks of the calm golden Suir,
　　　　　　　　Bright and pure,
　On the banks of the calm golden Suir.

II.

By upland springs a lonely linnet sings
　All of love, from his leafy wildwood tree,
Of smiles and sweet sighs, and the loving star-bright eyes
　That are gazing so fond now on me,
　　　　　　　　Trustingly,
　That are gazing so fond now on me!

III.

The soft airs blow, and wildly wandering go
　To tell, where the woodlark builds its nest,
Of bliss that knows no care, and the maiden young and fair,
　That I'm clasping so fond to my breast,
　　　　　　　　Dearly pressed,
　That I'm clasping so fond to my breast.

IV.

Oh! bright flow the rills and this river by the hills,
   Telling, telling as they go to mount and moor
That my love's at my side, that she'll be my own
     dear bride,
   On the banks of the calm golden Suir,
                Bright and pure,
   On the banks of the calm golden Suir.

SONG OF GALLOPING O'HOGAN.

AIR—"He thought of the charmer".

I.

Hurra! boys, hurra! for the sword by my side,
The spur and the gallop o'er bogs deep and wide,—
Hurra! for the helmet and shinin' steel jack,
The sight of the spoil and good men at my back!
    And we'll sack and burn for king and sireland,
    And chase the black foe from ould Ireland!

II.

At the wave of my sword start a thousand good
   men,
And we ride like the blast over moorland and glen;
Like dead leaves of winter, in ruin and wrath
We sweep the red Saxons away from our path,
    And we'll sack and burn for king and sireland,
    And chase the black foe from ould Ireland!

III.

The herds of the foe graze at noon by the rills:
We have them at night in our camp 'mid the hills:

His towns lie in peace at the eve of the night;
But they're sacked and in flames ere the next
  mornin' light!
    And we'll sack and burn for king and sireland,
    And chase the black foe from ould Ireland!

IV.

And so we go ridin' by night and by day,
And fight for our country and all the rich prey;
The roar of the battle sweet music we feel,
And the light of our hearts is the flashin' of steel!
    And we'll sack and burn for king and sireland,
    And chase the black foe from ould Ireland!

FANNY.

Air—"Royal Charlie".

I.

Where Anner flows by fairy rath
  And tower and gray rocks many,
One Sunday noon in woodland path
  I met my blithesome Fanny.
Her hair was like the yellow blooms
  That deck the meadows early;
Her eyes like heaven, when spring illumes,
  They shone so kind and clearly.

II.

We sat to hear the river's tune
  'Neath trees all mossed and olden,
And talked and laughed that autumn noon,
  With thoughts full sweet and golden;—

I built a palace in my brain
    As fond I gazed upon her,
And in its bright halls she did reign,
    My queen of love and honour!

III.

The palace towers may all depart,
    And cruel fate may sever,
But in my brain and in my heart
    Her form shall live for ever;—
At beauty's shrine the worshippers
    Judge fond and rash and blindly;
Yet ne'er was form more fair than hers,
    And ne'er beat heart more kindly.

THE END.

J. F. Fowler, Printer, 3 Crow Street, Dame Street, Dublin.

www.ingramcontent.com/pod-product-compliance
Lightning Source LLC
Chambersburg PA
CBHW022106230426
43672CB00008B/1302